No doubt this year, like every year, thousands of students will be 'starting Shakespeare'.

Painstakingly they'll be going through their copies of the plays, making their acquaintance with the well-known names in Shakespeare's dramatic gallery: Macbeth, Viola, Romeo and Juliet, Julius Caesar, Shylock, Prince Hal, Bottom the Weaver – and dozens more.

They may be wondering: who was this man Shakespeare? Why have his plays lasted so long? Where were they first performed? Who acted in them? Are they really 'great'?

We'll try to answer some of these questions by imagining that we can interview some of the people most closely associated with Shakespeare's life and work. Through their answers to our questions, we'll piece together a picture of Shakespeare the man and the theatre he wrote for. But let's begin one step back – with William's father, John Shakespeare.

Son of a tenant farmer, he lived at Snitterfield in Warwickshire. Probably never went to school. Served his time as a glover. Eventually started a business in Stratford upon Avon selling gloves and leather articles from his house in Henley Street and from a local market stall.

Married Mary Arden, youngest daughter of Robert Arden who owned the farm on which John had been brought up.

He was soon involved in local affairs. First he became a councillor – one of his jobs being to taste the ale to make sure it was up to strength!

Then he became one of the town constables who did their nightly rounds to pick up the odd drunkard, catch a prowling thief and make sure the citizens were keeping the peace.

Was promoted to chamberlain and was in charge of the town's finances; then to alderman and finally to high bailiff – Stratford's chief citizen.

In the meantime he had become the father of a large family. His first son he names William. William Shakespeare makes his entrance. We'll let John Shakespeare take up the story from there.

An Interview with
JOHN SHAKESPEARE

INTERVIEWER

Good evening Mr Shakespeare. Will you forgive me if I begin with one of the oldest questions in the book? What was it like to be the father of the world's most famous dramatist?

JOHN

If you must know, it was much like being the father of any normal, healthy, intelligent boy, who often got into trouble and took his beatings like anyone else.

INTERVIEWER

But he must have had a special place in your affections when he was very young – not because he was clever, but because your first two children had died in infancy, I believe.

JOHN

Yes, Joan and Margaret. Will was our third, born in the April of 1564 when the plague was at its height. There were over two hundred deaths in Stratford alone between the July and the December – many of them children. We thanked the Lord that Will was spared.

INTERVIEWER

And after Will?

JOHN

Will was our first, you might say. Then came Gilbert, Joan – the second Joan, that is – Anne, Richard and Edmund. Edmund was full sixteen years younger than Will.

INTERVIEWER

Eldest sons used to follow in their father's footsteps in your day, I think. Did William help you in your business and your other duties?

JOHN

He grew up knowing all about my trade as a glover, but I didn't insist that he followed me in it. And he learnt a lot about constables and bailiffs too when he was at home; but Will had a mind of his own – and a better one than mine! He wasn't going to follow in his father's footsteps.

INTERVIEWER

Well, I suppose he had already started off in a new direction by going to the King's New School, the grammar school in Stratford upon Avon. Did he like it? Or was he like the schoolboy in one of his speeches – 'creeping like snail unwillingly to school'?

JOHN

Like all the boys, he was glad when home-time came! Yes, they worked them hard at that school, especially at their Latin and Greek.

INTERVIEWER

We know that students in Elizabethan times used to read the Bible in Greek. Do you remember Will doing that?

JOHN

Yes, I do. And those Roman dramatists in Latin. What were their names now?

INTERVIEWER

Seneca and Plautus?

JOHN

Aye, that sounds something like . . . Seneca . . . and . . . Plautus . . . yes . . .

INTERVIEWER

He obviously had a good grounding in the classical authors, as we can see from his frequent references to them in his plays. But what about the school day itself? What time did school begin?

JOHN

He had to be up at half-past five in the morning in summer to be at school for six o'clock, though it became seven in winter. They had a break for breakfast, then lessons till eleven. Will's school was only a quarter of a mile from our house in Henley Street and he used to come home to dinner. Afternoon school began at one o'clock and went on till five. Six days a week that was, with two afternoons off.

INTERVIEWER

Hm! We've eased up a little since then. Perhaps that's

4

why we're not producing so many Shakespeares!

JOHN
One is enough!

INTERVIEWER
Yet many people have argued that because your son left school when he was fifteen and grew up in such a quiet, remote town in rural England, he couldn't possibly have written the remarkable plays we call Shakespeare's.

JOHN
Well, I can't say I'm surprised! We found it hard to believe ourselves at first, but then we got used to the idea of Will being famous and successful. Mind you, it was London that developed his talents, not Stratford, though he was not slow to mature, even in rural England!

INTERVIEWER
Which brings us on to his marriage. William, aged eighteen, married Anne Hathaway, aged twenty-six, and six months later their first child is born. All the world knows the story. One half says 'tut, tut!' and the other says 'He must have been quite a lad, this Shakespeare!' What did you say?

66 must have been quite a lad 99

JOHN
I'd better not repeat what I said! But he did the honourable thing, he married her; and when Susanna was born, she became a playmate for Will's youngest brother, Edmund, who was no more than three at the time! Then, less than two years later, Anne gave birth to the twins, Hamnet and Judith.

INTERVIEWER
So by the time he was twenty, Will was the father of three children! Living with you in Henley Street?

JOHN
Yes, living at home, but longing to get away.

INTERVIEWER
You mean Stratford was too small for a man of his talents?

JOHN
Yes, he was restless. London was the place. Everything was happening there and the acting companies that came to Stratford in the summer months gave Will a taste of what it would be like to perform in London. There was no holding him. Wife and children or no – he was away – joined one of the companies and began a new life! Caused problems that did! But you must remember that he didn't desert us altogether. He came back often. Never lost his ties with his family or Stratford.

INTERVIEWER
One more question, Mr Shakespeare, if I may. It's about his reasons for leaving Stratford. One story – or rumour, or tradition – has it that he fled Stratford because he was charged with stealing deer from the park of Sir Thomas Lucy. It sounds very unlikely, I know, but how much truth is there in it?

JOHN
None at all! Mind you, I wouldn't have put it past Will – but the fact is that Sir Thomas Lucy didn't have a licence to keep deer, so there were none to steal! That story's a rumour. No, Will left Stratford for mightier reasons than stealing deer!

INTERVIEWER
And when we next hear of him, he was an actor, a poet and a dramatist. But what happened to him in the intervening years has remained a mystery. They are sometimes called 'the lost years' and I would dearly love to ask you about them, Mr Shakespeare.

JOHN
And I would dearly love to tell you, but that would be breaking the rules, wouldn't it? And we can't do that!

INTERVIEWER
No, I suppose we can't. They'll just have to remain 'the lost years' and we'll have to draw our interview to a close. But for all you have told us about William, thank you very much, Mr Shakespeare.

JOHN
Thank you. Now I can go back to my quiet little corner in history. Besides, why bother with what I have to say when you have Will's plays themselves?

PRESENTER
But we cannot leave this early period of Shakespeare's life without mentioning his poems. Some time after his arrival in London he acquired a patron – a wealthy young aristocrat named Henry Wriothesley, third Earl of Southampton, to whom he dedicated his long narrative poems 'Venus and Adonis' and 'The Rape of Lucrece'. In return he received financial support and artistic encouragement from his patron. But though the poems were popular and ran into several editions, Shakespeare was obviously finding the life of a dramatist more absorbing than the life of a pure poet; and soon the patron fades into the background and the theatre takes over completely.

CHECKPOINT

Twenty quick questions for oral or written answers, based on the interview with John Shakespeare.

1 What was John Shakespeare's occupation?
2 In which street in Stratford upon Avon did he live?
3 What was the maiden name of Shakespeare's mother?
4 What was one of the functions of a councillor in Stratford then?
5 What job did a constable do?
6 What responsibility did a chamberlain have?
7 What was the highest position John Shakespeare rose to in Stratford?
8 How many children had John and Mary Shakespeare?
9 Where did William come in the family?
10 Which school did William go to?
11 Which languages did he study?
12 What time did the school begin in summer?
13 How long was the school day?
14 How old was William when he got married?
15 How old was Anne Hathaway at the time?
16 What was the name of their first child?
17 What were the names of the twins?
18 What name is given to the period between Shakespeare's leaving Stratford and his appearance in London as an actor and a poet?
19 What were the titles of Shakespeare's narrative poems?
20 Who was his patron at this time?

I SAID IT!

There is a story that an old lady went to a performance of *Hamlet* and came away complaining that the play was full of quotations.

She was right. A great many words and expressions from *Hamlet* – as well as from the other plays – have caught on and become part of our everyday English.

A well-known television series, starring Penelope Keith, was called 'To the Manor Born', which was a variation on **To the manner born**, from *Hamlet*.

A blinking idiot is a phrase used in *The Merchant of Venice* to describe a portrait.

Punk was first used by Shakespeare in *The Merry Wives of Windsor*, though it had a slightly different meaning to its modern one!

Why is **To be or not to be** the best-known quotation in the English language? What does it mean? Who said it?

We've all heard of someone 'laying it on with a trowel'. It comes from **Laid on with a trowel** in *As You Like It*.

'What the dickens!' has nothing to do with Charles, the novelist. It originates in **I cannot tell what the dickens his name is** in *The Merry Wives of Windsor*.

'As luck would have it' was originally **As good luck would have it** – from the same play.

'All that glitters is not gold' was originally **All that glisters is not gold** in *The Merchant of Venice*.

A few years ago there were widespread strikes during the winter months and the period is now often referred to as 'the winter of discontent', from **Now is the winter of our discontent** (*King Richard III*).

When you say something has **Seen better days**, you are quoting from *Timon of Athens*.

'She looked daggers' comes from Hamlet's saying **I will speak daggers to her, but use none.**

'It's Greek to me' began with Casca saying in *Julius Caesar* **It was Greek to me.**

The Hostess in *Henry IV, Part 2*, complains of Falstaff: **He hath eaten me out of house and home** – and adds **he hath put all my substance into that fat belly of his.**

It is often the quotations that seem to express a general truth that have remained popular. Can you find out where these sayings originated?

A rose by any other name would smell as sweet.
Give the devil his due.
Parting is such sweet sorrow.
It's a wise father that knows his own child.
Brevity is the soul of wit.

SPEAK THE SPEECH

Some people find it very difficult to read Shakespeare aloud; others love it. There's no doubt, however, that the better the reading, the more the play will be enjoyed and understood by both readers and listeners.

Let us assume that so far you have not actually read anything by Shakespeare, but that you are prepared to begin. You will be helped if you remember these points:

1. Emphasise the words you think are important.

2. Pause at commas, semi-colons and full-stops.

3. If there is no stop at the end of a line, read straight on to the next line.

4. -ed at the end of a word is pronounced as a separate syllable:
advis-ed   inform-ed   trench-ed.
If the full syllable is not to be pronounced, an apostrophe is used:
advis'd   inform'd   trench'd.

5. Try to give expression to the *feelings* of the characters.

6. Wherever possible, convey these feelings by your tone of voice, your facial expression, your gestures and your movements.

7. Don't rush to get through the speech – take your time!

Here are some short quotations and extracts to practise on, arranged under headings. If you can enjoy speaking these, you will enjoy the longer speeches when they come.

INSULTS

In *A Midsummer Night's Dream*, Lysander uses Hermia's size to insult her:
Get you gone, you dwarf
Where would the pause come?
Which word would be said with most force?
What expression would be on Lysander's face?
What movements could he make?
What is he feeling?

In *Romeo and Juliet*, Capulet gets angry with his daughter Juliet because she refuses to marry the man he has chosen for her:

Hang thee, young baggage! disobedient wretch!
I tell thee what – get thee to church a Thursday,
Or never after look me in the face.

Which words would be stressed?
How loudly do you think the speech ought to be said?

Would all the pauses be of the same length?
What tone of voice would Capulet use?
Should he be sitting, standing, walking about, gesturing?

Ask yourself similar questions for the following quotations, then try speaking them:

- **Away, you mouldy rogue, away!**

- **I dote upon his very absence**

- **Not Hercules could have knocked his brains out, for he had none!**

- *Jaques.* **Let's meet as little as we can.**
  Orlando. **I do desire we may be better strangers.**

- **Would thou wert clean enough to spit upon!**

- **I have seen better faces in my time
  Than stands on any shoulder that I see
  Before me at this instant.**

MURDER & DEATH

One of Macbeth's hired-men comes to report Banquo's murder. Macbeth asks him if Banquo is 'safe':

Murderer. **Safe in a ditch he bides,
With twenty trenched gashes on his head.**

The murderer would be a tough, coarse man. What sort of voice would he have? He would probably speak slowly and firmly.
In the first line *safe* and *ditch* would be stressed and in the second line *twenty trenched gashes*.
Could there be a chuckle after *bides*?

Now try these on the same theme:

✳ Also from *Macbeth*. Macduff rushes in with the news of King Duncan's murder:

**Awake, awake!
Ring the alarum bell. Murder and treason!**

✳ Lady Macbeth, sleepwalking, dreams that she still has the blood of Duncan on her hands:

Here's the smell of blood still. All the perfumes of Arabia will not sweeten this little hand. Oh, oh, oh!

✳ Brutus, one of the assassins of Julius Caesar, delivers a speech to the Roman citizens in which he justifies his action:

As Caesar lov'd me, I weep for him; as he was fortunate, I rejoice at it; as he was valiant, I

honour him; but — as he was ambitious, I slew him. There is tears for his love; joy for his fortune; honour for his valour; and death for his ambition.

✳ Mercutio has been injured in a sword-fight. Romeo thinks it is just a scratch, but Mercutio knows he is about to die from it.

Romeo. **Courage, man; the hurt cannot be much.**
Mercutio. **No, 'tis not so deep as a well, nor so wide as a church door, but 'tis enough, 'twill serve. Ask for me to-morrow, and you shall find me a grave man.**

✳ During a battle scene in *Henry IV, Part I*, the Prince sees his old companion lying on the ground, apparently dead:

Prince. (spying Falstaff on the ground)
**What, old acquaintance! Could not all this flesh
Keep in a little life? Poor Jack, farewell!
I could have better spar'd a better man.**

LOVE & MARRIAGE

Love is a constant theme in Shakespeare's plays, but it is not always romantic love — it can be humorous as well! Think about the feelings of the characters in these quotations before acting out the lines yourself.

✳ From *A Midsummer Night's Dream*:

O dainty duck!

✳ Romeo, before he has met Juliet, protests that no-one could possibly be as beautiful as his present love, Rosaline:

**One fairer than my love! The all-seeing sun
Ne'er saw her match since first the world begun.**

❋ King Henry V, having defeated France in battle, proposes marriage to the French princess, Katherine:

Katherine. **Is it possible dat I sould love de enemy of France?**

King. **No, it is not possible you should love the enemy of France, Kate, but in loving me you should love the friend of France; for I love France so well that I will not part with a village of it; I will have it all mine. And, Kate, when France is mine and I am yours, then yours is France and you are mine.**

Katherine. **I cannot tell vat is dat.**

❋ In *The Taming of the Shrew* Petruchio speaks enthusiastically about Katherina:

Now, by the world, it is a lusty wench;
I love her ten times more than e'er I did.
O, how I long to have some chat with her.

and later, Gremio describes the wedding kiss:

This done, he took the bride about the neck,
And kiss'd her lips with such a clamorous smack
That at the parting all the church did echo.

❋ Phebe, a country lass, falls in love with Rosalind, disguised as a boy:

Rosalind. **Why look you so upon me?**
Phebe. **For no ill will I bear you.**
Rosalind. **I pray you do not fall in love with me,**
   For I am falser than vows made in wine;
   Besides, I like you not.

❋ Back to *Romeo and Juliet*; Rosaline forgotten, Romeo parts from Juliet:

Juliet. **Romeo!**
Romeo. **My dear?**
Juliet. **At what o'clock to-morrow**
   Shall I send to thee?
Romeo. **By the hour of nine.**
Juliet. **I will not fail. 'Tis twenty years till then.**

GETTING THE SOUND RIGHT

Here are a few miscellaneous quotations which you might enjoy saying. Don't worry if you can't understand them — just make them sound right!

Away, you scullion! you rampallion! you
   fustilarian!
I'll tickle your catastrophe!

I did impeticos thy gratillity.

   Bloody, bawdy villain!
Remorseless, treacherous, lecherous, kindless
   villain!

TWO PORTRAITS

What did Shakespeare look like?

There are hundreds of portraits of him, but only two can claim to be true likenesses.
They are known as the Droeshout engraving and the Chandos portrait.

A The Droeshout Engraving

After Shakespeare's death some of his friends decided to publish his plays in a collected edition.

They commissioned Martin Droeshout, an engraver, to engrave a portrait of Shakespeare to appear as a frontispiece.

Martin was only 15 when Shakespeare died and 22 when the engraving appeared. It is unlikely that he ever sketched Shakespeare from life.

The editors of the collected works said the engraving was an excellent likeness; but others have said it has glaring faults.

B The Chandos Portrait

This is an oil painting of Shakespeare by an unknown artist and named after Lord Chandos, who once owned it.

In the seventeenth century, it belonged to Thomas Betterton, a famous Shakespearean actor.

Before that it was owned by Sir William Davenant, whose father had been the landlord of a wine-shop in Oxford where Shakespeare used to stay on his journeys from London to Stratford. William Davenant was Shakespeare's godson and it is probably no coincidence that they share the same Christian name.

What do you think?

- On the evidence given above, which of these portraits is more likely to be a true likeness of Shakespeare?
- Study the details of the portraits. What similarities are there? What differences?
- Does it matter whether we know what Shakespeare looked like?
- Which of the portraits do you prefer?
- Can you find any other portraits of Shakespeare?

DOGBERRY SETS THE WATCH

from *Much Ado About Nothing*

The story takes place in Italy, but this scene is obviously set in the heart of Elizabethan England.

DOGBERRY, the Chief Constable, is choosing a deputy and giving the watch his advice before they set off on their night rounds. His advice is to avoid trouble at all costs!

You will notice Dogberry's strange use of language, which includes oddities such as saying *desartless* (undeserving) when he means the opposite: *deserving; senseless* when he means *sensible, comprehend* when he means *apprehend* and *tolerable* when he means *intolerable!*

VERGES is a doddery old man and Dogberry's assistant.

FIRST WATCH } These are the 'special constables' whose
SECOND WATCH } liveliness and daring would be well
known by Elizabethan audiences!

A note on the language

Most editions of Shakespeare's plays contain notes explaining unusual words and phrases and it is best to glance at these before you begin reading. Gradually you will learn the meaning of commonly used Elizabethan words and abbreviations, some of which occur in this scene:

'a (ln. 24) = he   by'r (ln. 69) = by your   marry (ln. 71) = a mild oath; (Virgin)Mary

---

ACT 3, SCENE 3

A STREET

Enter DOGBERRY *and* VERGES, *with the* Watch.

DOGBERRY	Are you good men and true?	
VERGES	Yea, or else it were pity but they should suffer salvation, body and soul.	2 *salvation*: Verges means damnation
DOGBERRY	Nay, that were a punishment too good for them, if they should have any allegiance in them, being chosen for the Prince's watch.	5 5 *allegiance*: loyalty – but Dogberry means the opposite!
VERGES	Well, give them their charge, neighbour Dogberry.	
DOGBERRY	First, who think you the most desartless man to be constable?	8 *desartless*: undeserving – but Dogberry means 'deserving'
FIRST WATCH	Hugh Oatcake, sir, or George Seacoal; for they can write and read.	10
DOGBERRY	Come hither, neighbour Seacoal. God hath bless'd you with a good name. To be a well-favoured man is the gift of fortune; but to write and read comes by nature.	
SECOND WATCH	Both which, Master Constable—	15
DOGBERRY	You have; I knew it would be your answer. Well, for your favour, sir, why, give God thanks, and make no boast of it; and for your writing and reading, let that appear when there is no need of such vanity. You are thought here to be the most senseless and fit man for the constable of the watch; therefore bear you the lantern. This is your charge: you shall comprehend all vagrom men; you are to bid any man stand, in the Prince's name.	20 22 *vagrom*: vagrant; a Dogberryism
SECOND WATCH	How, if 'a will not stand?	
DOGBERRY	Why, then, take no note of him, but let him go; and	25

12

	presently call the rest of the watch together, and thank God you are rid of a knave.	
VERGES	If he will not stand when he is bidden, he is none of the Prince's subjects.	
DOGBERRY	True, and they are to meddle with none but the Prince's subjects. You shall also make no noise in the streets; for for the watch to babble and to talk is most tolerable and not to be endured.	30
SECOND WATCH	We will rather sleep than talk; we know what belongs to a watch.	35
DOGBERRY	Why, you speak like an ancient and most quiet watchman, for I cannot see how sleeping should offend; only, have a care that your bills be not stol'n. Well, you are to call at all the ale-houses, and bid those that are drunk get them to bed.	40
SECOND WATCH	How if they will not?	
DOGBERRY	Why, then, let them alone till they are sober; if they make you not then the better answer, you may say they are not the men you took them for.	
SECOND WATCH	Well, sir.	45
DOGBERRY	If you meet a thief, you may suspect him, by virtue of your office, to be no true man; and, for such kind of men, the less you meddle or make with them, why, the more is for your honesty.	
SECOND WATCH	If we know him to be a thief, shall we not lay hands on him?	50
DOGBERRY	Truly, by your office, you may, but I think they that touch pitch will be defil'd; the most peaceable way for you, if you do take a thief, is to let him show himself what he is, and steal out of your company.	55
VERGES	You have been always called a merciful man, partner.	
DOGBERRY	Truly, I would not hang a dog by my will, much more a man who hath any honesty in him.	
VERGES	If you hear a child cry in the night, you must call to the nurse and bid her still it.	60
SECOND WATCH	How if the nurse be asleep and will not hear us?	
DOGBERRY	Why, then, depart in peace, and let the child wake her with crying; for the ewe that will not hear her lamb when it baes will never answer a calf when he bleats.	
VERGES	'Tis very true.	65
DOGBERRY	This is the end of the charge: you, constable, are to present the Prince's own person; if you meet the Prince in the night, you may stay him.	
VERGES	Nay, by'r lady, that I think 'a cannot.	
DOGBERRY	Five shillings to one on't, with any man that knows the statues, he may stay him; marry, not without the Prince be willing; for, indeed, the watch ought to offend no man, and it is an offence to stay a man against his will.	70
VERGES	By 'r lady, I think it be so.	75
DOGBERRY	Ha, ah, ha! Well, masters, good night; an there be any matter of weight chances, call up me; keep your fellows' counsels and your own, and good night. Come, neighbour.	
SECOND WATCH	Well, masters, we hear our charge; let us go sit here upon the church bench till two, and then all to bed.	80
DOGBERRY	One word more, honest neighbours: I pray you watch about Signior Leonato's door; for the wedding being there to-morrow, there is a great coil to-night. Adieu; be vigitant, I beseech you.	85

[*Exeunt* DOGBERRY *and* VERGES.

38 *bills*: pikes

53 *defil'd*: made unclean

68 *stay*: stop

77 *matter of weight chances*: if anything serious happens

84 *coil*: bustle, commotion
85 *vigitant*: vigilant

13

FORUM

Shakespeare lived four hundred years ago. He couldn't possibly know anything about the life we lead in the twentieth century. Why should we read *his* plays when we could be reading modern ones that deal with life and problems of today?

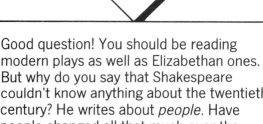

Good question! You should be reading modern plays as well as Elizabethan ones. But why do you say that Shakespeare couldn't know anything about the twentieth century? He writes about *people*. Have people changed all that much over the centuries? They still kill one another, fall in love, start revolutions, get bored, angry, jealous, drunk – children still quarrel with their parents, husbands and wives still have rows and leave each other – as they do in Shakespeare.

There's racial prejudice in *The Merchant of Venice,* political assassination in *Julius Caesar* and *Macbeth*, teenage marriage and suicide in *Romeo and Juliet* – it's amazing what Shakespeare knew about the problems that occupy us in the twentieth century!

DO YOU AGREE?
Has human nature remained the same? What twentieth-century situations and problems could not be presented in Shakespeare?

Do you think someone like Shakespeare, who probably left school when he was about fifteen, got married when he was eighteen and then turned up in London as an actor – do you think he *could* have written all those plays? He can't have been very well educated, can he?

Why not?
Do you have to go to university to be a genius?

Bernard Shaw was one of the greatest dramatists of modern times – he considered himself at least as good as Shakespeare – and he educated himself after he left school. Why couldn't Shakespeare do the same?

There's an interesting parallel in Shakespeare's own day. A gentleman named R. Willis – born the same year as Shakespeare – went to a free grammar school, as Shakespeare did – and eventually became secretary to the Chancellor of the Exchequer and to the Lord-keeper of the Great Seal. Why couldn't William Shakespeare become a successful dramatist from the same beginnings?

Can you think of other famous people who left school at an early age?
What exactly is 'genius'? Does the success of Shakespeare and Shaw mean that we don't need education after we've left school?

An Interview with
RICHARD BURBAGE

PRESENTER
At the age of 28 – five years after leaving Stratford – William Shakespeare had become a well-known figure in the theatrical world of London. He was in at the beginning of a great period of theatrical history in England, when writing, acting and theatre design were developing in new and exciting directions. One of the leading figures in the theatrical world of the day was Richard Burbage – a lifelong friend and business associate of Shakespeare's. He is the subject of our next interview.

INTERVIEWER
It's an honour to meet you, Mr Burbage. I read recently that audiences in the Elizabethan theatre always called the actors by their Christian names. So you were known as Richard?

BURBAGE
No, I was Dick. Dick Burbage. Your William Shakespeare was Will. We didn't stand on ceremony!

INTERVIEWER
Both in your twenties, both seeking success in London, both with an interest in the theatre –

BURBAGE
In acting, at first. As time went on, Will took to writing plays, whilst I remained an actor. I had acting in my blood, from my father, James Burbage. You've heard of James Burbage, haven't you?

INTERVIEWER
Of course – James Burbage. He built the first theatre. He set the ball rolling!

BURBAGE
And he called it The Theatre – as it was – the only one. In Finsbury Fields, outside the City walls. Not only did he build the first theatre, he made his audiences pay at the door before they saw the play.

INTERVIEWER
Brilliant! But what had happened before? Were performances free?

BURBAGE
No, not free. They just passed the box round and if you felt like putting something in, you did! If the play was a flop, no one gave anything! Not a very profitable way to run a theatre!

INTERVIEWER
Your father seems to have been the founder of the commercial theatre – and it survives to this day!

BURBAGE
And he did very well out of his new system – until the lease of The Theatre ran out and the landlord, Giles Allen, refused to renew it. He hated everything to do with plays and players and said he wanted to put his land to better use. But we weren't going to be defeated by *him*! So we waited till he was out of town and my brother Cuthbert and I, plus a theatre carpenter and a dozen workmen, took the theatre apart, timber by timber, loaded it on carts, transported it over the Thames and a year later we had built The Globe on Bankside, where most of

Will's great plays were performed.

INTERVIEWER
Had you kept up your friendship with Will since you had been actors together?

BURBAGE
Oh, yes. We were members of the same acting company, the Lord Chamberlain's Men.

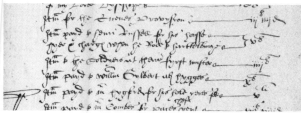

Manuscript of household accounts showing a payment made to a group of players

INTERVIEWER
Perhaps we had better have that explained. Who were the Lord Chamberlain's Men?

BURBAGE
One of the companies of actors found in and around London. Each company had a patron and was licensed by him to perform plays. Our patron was the Lord Chamberlain and, of course, we used to perform for him privately as well as act in the public theatres.

INTERVIEWER
Wasn't the company a business as well? Weren't you aiming at making a good living out of acting?

BURBAGE
We did it for love *and* money – it's a combination that never fails! Will and I were shareholders in the company and in The Globe. Our artistic and our financial success went hand in hand!

INTERVIEWER
And the great parts you created at The Globe – Lear, Hamlet, Othello, Macbeth – were money-spinners for you and for Shakespeare?

BURBAGE
They earned us a lot of money, if that's what you mean!

INTERVIEWER
There's a story that Shakespeare himself played the Ghost to your Hamlet.

66 We did it for love *and* money 99

BURBAGE
He did, of course he did! Will was a *very* fine actor – in the minor roles! He was a wonderful Adam in *As You Like It* – and he was a first-rate comedian! Will was very versatile.

INTERVIEWER
Did he ever act before Queen Elizabeth?

The exterior of the Barbican

The interior of the Barbican

BURBAGE

Yes, quite often. The Queen was very fond of Will's plays and, naturally, as one of the company, he acted in them himself.

INTERVIEWER

What happened when the Queen died and James 1 took over? Were the Lord Chamberlain's Men still popular?

BURBAGE

More popular than ever! He adopted us as his own troupe of actors. We ceased to be the Lord Chamberlain's Men and became the King's Men. I remember to this day the words of our royal patent. It licensed . . . 'these our servants Lawrence Fletcher, William Shakespeare, Richard Burbage . . . and the rest of their associates . . . freely to use and exercise the art of playing comedies, tragedies, histories, interludes, morals, pastorals, stage-plays . . . as well for the recreation of our loving subjects as for our pleasure when we shall think good to see them . . .'

INTERVIEWER

Whew! What a memory you have, Mr Burbage! If the king was your patron, does that mean you were part of the royal household?

BURBAGE

Of course! Each of us received four and half yards of scarlet red cloth for our livery.

INTERVIEWER

You really had made it to the top, as we would say nowadays! Did your court performances shoot up?

BURBAGE

From an average of three a year to thirteen a year — more than all other London companies combined. And why? Because the king enjoyed *The Comedy of Errors, Love's Labour's Lost, The Merry Wives of Windsor, The Merchant of Venice* — as well as the great tragedies.

INTERVIEWER

He must also have enjoyed the actors who performed the plays – not least, yourself. It was obviously a great partnership: Shakespeare the writer and you the actor. One could not have been as successful without the other.

BURBAGE

My talent served his genius!

INTERVIEWER

We shall never know how modest you are being, Mr Burbage, because his plays have survived, but – to our deep regret – your performances are lost to us. I wonder, if you were to see a modern production of one of Shakespeare's plays, whether you would see a great change in interpretation since your day?

BURBAGE

What are the chances of my seeing one of Will's plays before I return? *Hamlet? Lear? Othello?*

INTERVIEWER

Well, as it happens, there *is* a performance of *Hamlet* at the Barbican tonight and I have two tickets. Would you care to come along?

BURBAGE

I'd love to! I wonder who'll be playing the Ghost!

CHECKPOINT

Questions for oral or written answers, based on the interview with Richard Burbage.

1 What had Richard Burbage and William Shakespeare in common?

2 James Burbage, Richard's father, introduced two new ideas into the sixteenth century London theatrical world. What were they?

3 Explain how The Globe on Bankside came to be built.

4 Which acting company did Burbage and Shakespeare belong to?

5 What was one of the functions of a theatrical patron?

6 Which four famous tragic roles in Shakespeare's plays were first performed by Richard Burbage?

7 Which part is Shakespeare thought to have played in *Hamlet*?

8 What became of the Lord Chamberlain's Men when Queen Elizabeth died?

9 What was the average annual number of royal performances given by Shakespeare's company under King James?

10 Can you name five plays that King James particularly enjoyed?

A GUIDED TOUR OF

including other famous sights and entertainments

1 The Theatre. First public theatre to be built specially for the performance of plays. Opened in 1576.

2 The Curtain. Second theatre to be built. Opened in 1577.

3 Walk half a mile to the wall surrounding the City of London. Enter by Bishop's Gate. The City authorities disapproved of theatres. We shall find only one within the City boundary.

4 Down Bishopsgate Street to Gracechurch Street. The Cross Keys Inn. Before (and after) the building of The Theatre, plays were acted in the courtyards of inns such as this one.

5 Along Cheapside to St Paul's – largest and most magnificent cathedral in England (but not the one

built by Sir Christopher Wren between 1675 and 1710). The choirboys are actors as well as singers. They are called The Children of the Chapel and perform at the nearby Blackfriars Theatre.

6 The Blackfriars Theatre. A private, indoor theatre – the only one licensed by the City authorities. Entrance fee is six times that of the public theatres. The King's Men acted here from 1609. Nearby: Blackfriar's Gate-house, bought by Shakespeare in 1613, but he never lived there.

7 Down to Puddle Wharf and river trip to the Tower of London.

8 Visit the Tower. See the Crown Jewels, armoury, Traitor's Gate and Bloody Tower. Visit menagerie in Lion Tower.

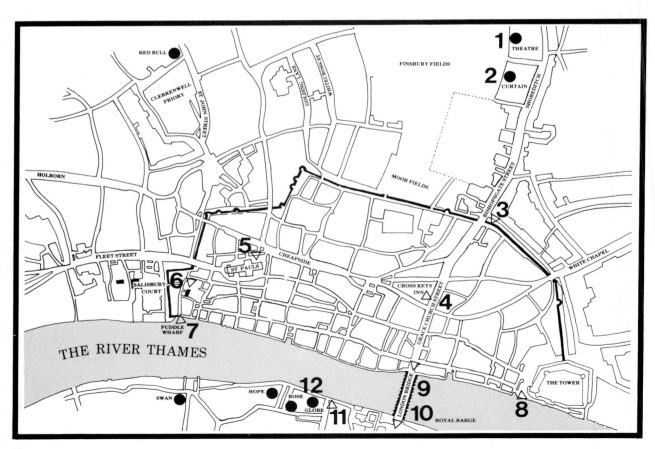

ELIZABETHAN THEATRES

Follow your route on the map and read the notes as you go.

9 Cross London Bridge. Half an hour free time for shopping on the Bridge and admiring merchants' houses above shops. Meet at gate-house on south side to see heads of executed criminals stuck on iron spikes.

10 Inspect Royal Barge moored on south bank of Thames.

11 South Bank entertainments: bear-baiting and bull-baiting amphitheatres; recreation in meadows if desired, including running, wrestling, archery, football, bowls and dancing round the maypole. Favourite picnic spot.

12 Elizabethan lunch in popular tavern before visit to The Globe for Shakespeare play in the afternoon (weather permitting).

LONDON THEATRES TODAY

- Compare the two maps of London in detail. What has remained unchanged for almost four centuries?
  What are the main changes?

- Try devising a modern theatrical tour (including famous sights and entertainments) for a group of Elizabethan tourists who are interested in our theatre. Give them some idea of modern theatrical entertainment by commenting on one or two plays and choose one to take them to at the end of the tour. You will find a list of 'What's On' in a daily newspaper.

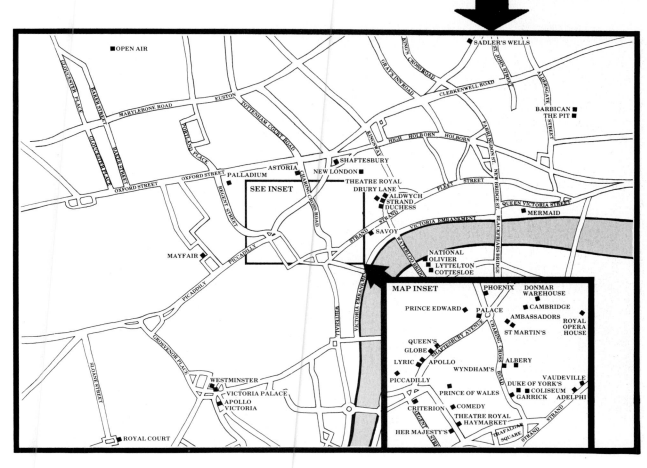

PRODUCTION NOTES

FOR THE OPENING OF
HAMLET

Burbage, as you have read, created the part of Hamlet, perhaps the best known of Shakespeare's characters.

The play tells the story of Hamlet, Prince of Denmark, who suspects that his father has been murdered by his uncle, Claudius, who then becomes king.

The play opens on the battlements of Elsinore Castle, just as Francisco is being relieved of his night watch by Bernardo, who is soon followed by Marcellus and Horatio.

Now for the past two nights, Bernardo and Marcellus have seen a ghost on the battlements. They have told Horatio, but he has ridiculed the idea, saying that it is just their imagination. They have persuaded him, however, to join them on their watch and see the ghost for himself. When it appears they recognise it as the ghost of the dead king.

A 'production exercise' is a detailed study of a text such as a producer would make to help his actors interpret their roles on the stage. Below is

an example of this kind of exercise on the opening lines of *Hamlet*. For any scene you are given, go through the following stages:

1 Read the extract, ignoring all the notes.
2 Read the text again, noting any words or lines that can be used as production clues. For example:

lines 1–2 | Bernardo and Francisco obviously cannot see each other. Stage should be in semi-darkness.

line 7 | **'Tis now struck twelve**
twelve strokes on bell (see line 39). Scene could open with these strokes.

line 8 | **'Tis bitter cold**
How can the coldness be suggested? Cloaks? Francisco shivering?

line 42 | **Well, sit we down,**
Horatio sits on steps, edge of platform or simply squats on the floor.

line 45 | **yond same star**
Lighting should suggest a starry night.

line 57 | **fair and warlike form**
line 72 | **the very armour he had on**
line 74 | **so frown'd he once**
line 79 | **martial stalk**
These lines indicate what the Ghost must look like – dressed in armour, frowning, walking with military stride – slow, powerful, but uneasy.

3 Go through the text again, making notes in the margin on movements, dramatic tension, words that need to be stressed, interpretation of character, etc.
4 Compare your production notes with another person's and discuss the differences. By now you will have a thorough knowledge of the scene and an understanding of the characters.

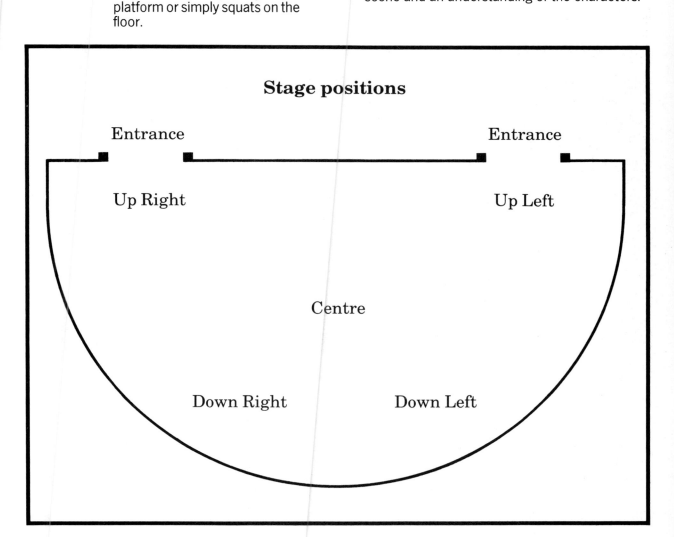

Stage positions

Entrance   Entrance

Up Right   Up Left

Centre

Down Right   Down Left

ACT 1, SCENE 1

ELSINORE. THE GUARD-PLATFORM OF THE CASTLE

OPENING - BARE STAGE
SEMI-DARKNESS
SILENCE
BELL CLANGS 12 TIMES

FRANCISCO *at his post. Enter to him* BERNARDO. *UP RIGHT*

CENTRE STAGE
ALERT AND NERVOUS

BERNARDO	Who's there?
FRANCISCO	Nay, answer me. Stand and unfold yourself. *TURNS QUICKLY- PEERS INTO SHADOWS* *TENSE DRAMATIC*
BERNARDO	Long live the King! *STRESS 'ME'*
FRANCISCO	Bernardo?
BERNARDO	He. *MOVING TO FRANCISCO* 5
FRANCISCO	You come most carefully upon your hour. *RELIEVED* *FRIENDLY COMRADELY TONE*
BERNARDO	'Tis now struck twelve; get thee to bed, Francisco. *SHIVERS -*
FRANCISCO	For this relief much thanks. 'Tis bitter cold, *LOOKS FED-UP*
	And I am sick at heart.
BERNARDO	Have you had quiet guard? 10
FRANCISCO	Not a mouse stirring.
BERNARDO	Well, good night.
	If you do meet Horatio and Marcellus,
	The rivals of my watch, bid them make haste.

14 rivals: partners

Enter HORATIO *and* MARCELLUS. *FROM UP R - FRANCISCO MEETS THEM*

SOUND OF FOOTSTEPS

FRANCISCO	I think I hear them. Stand, ho! Who is there? 15 *LOUD, MILITARY VOICE*
HORATIO	Friends to this ground.
MARCELLUS	And liegemen to the Dane.

17 liegeman: vassal, subject

FRANCISCO	Give you good night.
MARCELLUS	O, farewell, honest soldier! *SLAPS HIM ON SHOULDER*
	Who hath reliev'd you? 20
FRANCISCO	Bernardo hath my place.
	Give you good night. [*Exit.* *U R*
MARCELLUS	Holla, Bernardo!

MOVING DOWN CENTRE TO B.

BERNARDO	Say —
	What, is Horatio there? 25
HORATIO	A piece of him. *HORATIO'S HUMOUR*
BERNARDO	Welcome, Horatio; welcome, good Marcellus.
HORATIO	What, has this thing appear'd again to-night?
BERNARDO	I have seen nothing.
MARCELLUS	Horatio says 'tis but our fantasy, 30
	And will not let belief take hold of him
	Touching this dreaded sight, twice seen of us; *STRESS 'TWICE'*
	Therefore I have entreated him along
	With us to watch the minutes of this night,
	That, if again this apparition come, 35
	He may approve our eyes and speak to it.

JOINING THEM
HANDSHAKES
MOOD BECOMES MORE SERIOUS AND TENSE
CONTRAST MANNER OF H. (CASUAL DISBELIEVING) WITH EARNESTNESS OF M. AND B.
36 approve our eyes: confirm what we have seen

HORATIO	Tush, tush, 'twill not appear.
BERNARDO	Sit down awhile,
	And let us once again assail your ears,
	That are so fortified against our story, 40
	What we have two nights seen.
HORATIO	Well, sit we down, *SITS*
	And let us hear Bernardo speak of this.
BERNARDO	Last night of all,
	When yond same star that's westward from the pole 45
	Had made his course t' illume that part of heaven
	Where now it burns, Marcellus and myself,
	The bell then beating one —

WHILE THEY ARE LOOKING AT THE STAR, THE GHOST APPEARS UP L. WALKS IN SLOW MILITARY STYLE DOWN L.

Enter GHOST.

MARCELLUS	Peace, break thee off; look where it comes again.	
BERNARDO	In the same figure, like the King that's dead. 50	
MARCELLUS	Thou art a scholar; speak to it, Horatio.	
BERNARDO	Looks 'a not like the King? Mark it, Horatio.	
HORATIO	Most like. It harrows me with fear and wonder.	53 *harrows*: distresses
BERNARDO	It would be spoke to.	
MARCELLUS	Question it, Horatio. 55	
HORATIO	What art thou that usurp'st this time of night	56 *usurp'st*: unlaw-fully takes over
	Together with that fair and warlike form	
	In which the majesty of buried Denmark	
	Did sometimes march? By heaven I charge thee, speak!	
MARCELLUS	It is offended. 60	
BERNARDO	See, it stalks away.	
HORATIO	Stay! speak, speak! I charge thee, speak!	

[Exit GHOST.

MARCELLUS	'Tis gone, and will not answer.	
BERNARDO	How now, Horatio! You tremble and look pale.	
	Is not this something more than fantasy? 65	
	What think you on 't?	
HORATIO	Before my God, I might not this believe	68 *sensible*: through the senses
	Without the sensible and true avouch	68 *true avouch*: actual
	Of mine own eyes.	evidence
MARCELLUS	Is it not like the King? 70	
HORATIO	As thou art to thyself:	
	Such was the very armour he had on	
	When he the ambitious Norway combated;	73 *Norway*: King of Norway
	So frown'd he once when, in an angry parle,	74 *parle*: parley, argu-ment
	He smote the sledded Polacks on the ice. 75	75 *sledded Polacks*: Poles, who were on sledges
	'Tis strange.	
MARCELLUS	Thus twice before, and jump at this dead	77 *jump*: exactly
	hour,	79 *martial*: military
	With martial stalk hath he gone by our watch.	
HORATIO	In what particular thought to work I know not; 80	81 *gross and scope*: general drift
	But, in the gross and scope of mine opinion,	82 *bodes*: foretells
	This bodes some strange eruption to our state.	

PRODUCTION NOTES

FOR A SCENE FROM MACBETH

On their way back from a victorious battle, Macbeth and Banquo encounter three witches on a Scottish heath who prophesy that Macbeth will become, first, Thane of Glamis, then Thane of Cawdor, and finally King of Scotland.

Macbeth has already inherited the title Thane of Glamis, but how can he become Cawdor and ultimately king? Macbeth's imagination begins to work and ambition stirs in him when he learns that Cawdor has been condemned to death as a traitor and his title has been conferred on Macbeth. How can the next step be accomplished?

The short scene below describes Macbeth's meeting with the witches. Using the *Hamlet* exercise as a model, write production notes on it, making suggestions for such details as movements, lighting, costumes, dramatic tension, pace of dialogue, stress and interpretation of character.

ACT 1, SCENE 3

THREE WITCHES

THIRD WITCH	A drum, a drum! Macbeth doth come.	30
ALL	The Weird Sisters, hand in hand, Posters of the sea and land,	
		33 *Posters:* travellers
	Thus do go about, about; Thrice to thine, and thrice to mine,	35
	And thrice again, to make up nine. Peace! The charm's wound up.	
		37 *wound up:* completed
	Enter MACBETH *and* BANQUO.	
MACBETH	So foul and fair a day I have not seen.	

BANQUO	How far is 't call'd to Forres? What are these,	
	So wither'd, and so wild in their attire,	40
	That look not like th' inhabitants o' th' earth,	
	And yet are on 't? Live you, or are you aught	
	That man may question? You seem to understand me,	
	By each at once her choppy finger laying	
	Upon her skinny lips. You should be women,	45
	And yet your beards forbid me to interpret	
	That you are so.	
MACBETH	Speak, if you can. What are you?	
FIRST WITCH	All hail, Macbeth! Hail to thee, Thane of Glamis!	
SECOND WITCH	All hail, Macbeth! Hail to thee, Thane of Cawdor!	50
THIRD WITCH	All hail, Macbeth, that shalt be King hereafter!	
BANQUO	Good sir, why do you start, and seem to fear	
	Things that do sound so fair? I' th' name of truth,	
	Are ye fantastical, or that indeed	
	Which outwardly ye show? My noble partner	55
	You greet with present grace and great prediction	
	Of noble having and of royal hope,	
	That he seems rapt withal. To me you speak not.	
	If you can look into the seeds of time	
	And say which grain will grow and which will not,	60
	Speak then to me, who neither beg nor fear	
	Your favours nor your hate.	
FIRST WITCH	Hail!	
SECOND WITCH	Hail!	
THIRD WITCH	Hail!	65
FIRST WITCH	Lesser than Macbeth, and greater.	
SECOND WITCH	Not so happy, yet much happier.	
THIRD WITCH	Thou shalt get kings, though thou be none.	
	So, all hail, Macbeth and Banquo!	
FIRST WITCH	Banquo and Macbeth, all hail!	70
MACBETH	Stay, you imperfect speakers, tell me more.	
	By Sinel's death I know I am Thane of Glamis;	
	But how of Cawdor? The Thane of Cawdor lives,	
	A prosperous gentleman; and to be King	
	Stands not within the prospect of belief,	75
	No more than to be Cawdor. Say from whence	
	You owe this strange intelligence, or why	
	Upon this blasted heath you stop our way	
	With such prophetic greeting? Speak, I charge you.	
	[Witches vanish.	
BANQUO	The earth hath bubbles, as the water has,	80
	And these are of them. Whither are they vanish'd?	
MACBETH	Into the air; and what seem'd corporal melted	
	As breath into the wind. Would they had stay'd!	
BANQUO	Were such things here as we do speak about?	
	Or have we eaten on the insane root	85
	That takes the reason prisoner?	
MACBETH	Your children shall be kings.	
BANQUO	You shall be King.	
MACBETH	And Thane of Cawdor too; went it not so?	
BANQUO	To th' self-same tune and words. Who's here?	90
	Enter ROSS *and* ANGUS.	

39 *call'd*: said to be

44 *choppy*: chapped
45 *should be*: seem to be

52 *start*: jump

54 *fantastical*: imaginary
56 *grace*: title (i.e. Glamis)

61–62 *beg nor fear Your favours nor your hate*: neither beg your favours, nor fear your hate

68 *get*: beget

71 *imperfect*: puzzling, contradictory

77 *owe*: possess
77 *intelligence*: knowledge

85 *insane root*: a root that, when eaten, causes insanity

FORUM

When we read the Dogberry extract from *Much Ado About Nothing* we had to have notes to explain the difficult words. Why is Shakespeare's language so hard to understand? Couldn't he write in simple English? ....all the thees and thous...

Well, the English language has changed a lot in four centuries. Shakespeare's English probably *was* simpler to understand then than it is now.

Even so, the language *is* difficult because it is being used to say things that the average person couldn't express. When you have the gifts Shakespeare had, you want to use them – you don't want to stick to simple language and everyday expressions. It has been calculated that there are 29066 different words in Shakespeare's works!

It may be only when you *read* Shakespeare that you find the language difficult. On the stage, with the help of good actors who use voice and gesture and feeling to express character, it's surprising how much you can understand. Reading in class is a bit like a rehearsal in which you explore the text. It's not quite the real thing.

- ● Do you agree with these answers?
- ● Would it be better to see a performance of a Shakespeare play before reading it?
- ● Has the use of *thee* and *thou* completely disappeared from modern English?
- ● What can be said for reading or acting a simplified version of Shakespeare in which the language difficulties have been removed?

28

You hear people saying: 'Shakespeare said . . .' this and that, as though they were his opinions when really they are the opinions of his characters. Can anyone know what Shakespeare actually thought? What his opinions were?

No, not really. Scholars have tried to prove he was an arch conservative, a diehard protestant, a Roman Catholic, a mystic – all by quoting from the plays. But, as you say, it is the characters who speak, not Shakespeare. We don't know what his opinions were.

So you think we can't get to know anything about Shakespeare himself from reading his plays?

I'm not so sure. We may not know what he thought, but we have plenty of evidence of what he *knew*. He'd obviously read a great deal to develop his plots. He had a good knowledge of history, the law, wild flowers, hunting, leatherwork, animals – because he refers to all these expertly in his plays. He must have known a good deal about human nature too, from kings to clowns. He was probably humorous and witty, or he couldn't have written such good comedy. And a serious man because he wrote great tragedy. And a philosophic man because his plays are full of philosophy. You see, it's difficult to know where to stop!

● From the short passages you have read, what do you think can be deduced about Shakespeare that is not pure speculation?

● Does it matter whether or not we can get to know Shakespeare himself from the plays?

● Can you think of any dramatists or writers who deliberately aim to express their own point of view in their works?

SOME CHARACTERISTICS

The first set of quotations dealt with speaking Shakespeare's language. This group asks you to interpret meaning and to find some of the qualities that are characteristic of the plays — humour, wisdom, a knowledge of life and a command of language that is both rich and subtle.

Read the quotations and answer the short questions that follow them.

1

> look like th' innocent flower,
> But be the serpent under 't.
>
> (Lady Macbeth to Macbeth)

Lady Macbeth is advising her husband to kill the King. What exactly is she saying in this quotation?

2

> Light thickens, and the crow
> Makes wing to th' rooky wood;
> Good things of day begin to droop and drowse,
> Whiles night's black agents to their preys do rouse.
>
> (Macbeth)

What time of day is being described here?
Can you think of one example of 'night's black agents' and what its prey might be?

3

> Costly thy habit as thy purse can buy,
> But not express'd in fancy; rich, not gaudy;
> For the apparel oft proclaims the man;
>
> (Polonius in *Hamlet*)

Polonius is giving advice on clothes to his son who is about to leave Denmark for Paris. Put into your own words what he is saying .

4

> To die, to sleep;
> To sleep, perchance to dream. Ay, there's the rub;
> For in that sleep of death what dreams may come,
> When we have shuffled off this mortal coil,
> Must give us pause.
>
> (Hamlet)

This is a quotation from Hamlet's 'To be or not to be' speech in which he considers taking his own life. What is it, according to this quotation, which prevents him from committing suicide?

5

> All the world's a stage,
> And all the men and women merely players;
> They have their exits and their entrances;
> And one man in his time plays many parts,
> His acts being seven ages.
>
> (Jaques in *As You Like It*)

Which words continue the metaphor of the stage, expressed in the first line?
Put into your own words what Jaques means literally by 'exits and entrances'.

6 I saw a smith stand with his hammer, thus,
The whilst his iron did on the anvil cool,
With open mouth swallowing a tailor's news;
Who, with his shears and measure in his hand,
Standing on slippers, which his nimble haste
Had falsely thrust upon contrary feet,
Told of a many thousand warlike French
That were embattailed and rank'd in Kent.

(Hubert in *King John*)

Why does the smith let his iron cool?
What has happened to the tailor's slippers? Why?

7

What's gone and what's past help
Should be past grief.

(Paulina in *The Winter's Tale*)

Express in your own words what Paulina is saying here.

8 But look, the morn, in russet mantle clad,
Walks o'er the dew of yon high eastward hill.

(Horatio in *Hamlet*)

What figure of speech is Horatio using to describe which part of day?

9 Rich she shall be, that's certain; wise, or I'll none;
virtuous, or I'll never cheapen her; fair, or I'll never
look on her; mild, or come not near me; noble, or not I
for an angel; of good discourse, an excellent musician,
and her hair shall be of what colour it please God.

(Benedick in *Much Ado About Nothing*)

Benedick is describing his idea of the perfect woman. Make a list of the qualities he demands.

10 I'll have an action of battery against him, if there be
any law in Illyria; though I struck him first, yet it's
no matter for that.

(Sir Andrew in *Twelfth Night*)

Explain why this remark of Sir Andrew's would get a laugh in the theatre.

11 The man that hath no music in himself,
Nor is not mov'd with concord of sweet sounds,
Is fit for treasons, stratagems, and spoils;
The motions of his spirit are dull as night,
And his affections dark as Erebus.
Let no such man be trusted.

(Lorenzo in *The Merchant of Venice*)

What is Lorenzo's opinion of 'the man that hath no music in himself'?
Do you agree with his opinion?

An Interview with
THOMAS PLATTER

PRESENTER
From Mr Burbage, the great actor, to Mr Platter, an ordinary Elizabethan playgoer, one of the thousands who flocked to the theatres that had sprung up around the City of London, but particularly on the South Bank. Mr Thomas Platter is the subject of our next interview.

INTERVIEWER
Good afternoon, Mr Platter. It's extremely good . . .

THOMAS
Now before you begin, I just want to say that you mustn't ask me any difficult questions. I'm not an expert, and my memory's not as good as it was.

INTERVIEWER
Don't worry, Mr Platter, it'll be more like a conversation than an examination. I'll begin with an easy one. How did you actually get to The Globe?

THOMAS
That depended where I started from! When I first started going to The Globe I was an apprentice goldsmith, living by St Paul's. When I could afford it, I used to take a boat down the river to Bankside. When I was hard-up I walked across London Bridge – or rather I pushed and shoved my way across with crowds of others who were on their way to the South Bank.

32

INTERVIEWER

Were they all going to the theatres?

THOMAS

No. There were other entertainments besides watching plays – drinking in the taverns, for instance, cock-fighting, bull-baiting and bear-baiting. But I stuck to the theatres and my favourite theatre was The Globe. The Lord Chamberlain's Men ran it and they always had the best plays.

INTERVIEWER

What time did performances at The Globe begin?

THOMAS

About two o'clock. Dinner and a pot of ale, then to The Globe – that is, if the flag was flying. If it wasn't, it meant that bad weather had prevented the performance.

INTERVIEWER

Wasn't there a roof on the theatre?

THOMAS

Well, The Globe was really an eight-sided building with a little sloping thatched roof round the perimeter and the centre open to the sky.

INTERVIEWER

And when it rained, the audience got wet – hence the flag to warn people?

THOMAS

No, not quite! All the audience didn't get wet – only those in the belly. They were known as the 'groundlings'. Let me explain. It was a penny to go in –

INTERVIEWER

Thanks to Mr Burbage senior –

THOMAS

– and for one penny you could stand in the belly or the yard. This was the ground surrounding the stage. The people who stood there were called the 'groundlings'. It was they who got wet when it rained, because there was no roof over the yard. But surrounding the yard, forming the walls of the theatre, there were three circular galleries, the top one covered by the roof of thatch. It was a penny extra to get into the galleries.

INTERVIEWER

Was it worth paying the extra?

THOMAS

It certainly was! The lads in the belly could be a rough bunch of tinkers, and besides, it was hard on the feet, standing so long. In the gallery you got a seat, and a cushion, if you paid extra.

INTERVIEWER

Right, Thomas. We've got you in the gallery seat. You are sitting looking down at the stage. The play is about to begin. Tell us what you see.

THOMAS

First, the forepart of the stage thrusting into the yard, with the audience standing on three sides. At the back of the stage there is a curtained alcove called the 'tiring house' –

INTERVIEWER

What we would call the dressing room –

THOMAS

– and on either side of the tiring house there are doors through which the actors make their entrances and exits. Above the tiring house is the gallery for the musicians and for the rich young men who want to show off their feathered hats and fine clothes. Some of them have bought stools for sixpence and sit on the stage itself. What a nuisance these fops are. They interrupt the actors in their speeches, talk amongst themselves and walk out in the middle of a scene if the play displeases them!

INTERVIEWER

But this gallery above the tiring house: is it also used by the actors to present scenes in the play?

THOMAS

Of course. It was used for the balcony scene in *Romeo and Juliet* and I remember its being used for an upper window and the battlements of a town wall, just as the alcove below could represent an inner room, a cave or a prison cell.

INTERVIEWER

What is there above the balcony?

THOMAS

Above the balcony is the hut – like a tiny house popping its head over the walls of the theatre. Here is kept the suspension gear used for flying effects, and here the flag is hoisted to announce the performance.

INTERVIEWER

Was the stage itself covered – or do the actors suffer with the groundlings in bad weather?

THOMAS

It depended where the actors were standing. You see, two columns rise from the stage and support a canopy over the rear part of the stage in front of the tiring house, but the forepart of the stage is open to the heavens. If an actor stood there, he got wet! Or he ran for cover!

INTERVIEWER

It was a very adaptable stage, then. The actors could perform on the forepart of the stage, or under the canopy between the pillars, or in the alcove, or from the balcony.

THOMAS

Or they could come up through the trapdoor in the centre of the stage – a favourite entrance for ghosts!

INTERVIEWER

It seems to have been a theatre of action and movement. Was this your impression – that there was always something exciting happening on stage?

THOMAS

No, it wasn't. Sometimes the speeches were too long and the language was too difficult and the audience got very restless. But at other times, the actors held the eyes and ears of everyone in the house, or they had us collapsing with laughter.

INTERVIEWER

Why do you think Shakespeare's plays were so popular?

THOMAS

Why, there were plays to suit every taste – histories, comedies, tragedies, romances and sometimes a mixture of them all! Some went to see the murders, the swordfights, the battles and the cruel deaths. Some liked the slapstick comedy. Some went for the grand stories of Greece and Rome, the plays about Julius Caesar, Mark Antony and Cleopatra. Some liked the magical effects, the monsters and ghosts and witches. Some liked the love stories. I liked them all! I could never have enough.

INTERVIEWER

Shakespeare is treated very reverently today, both by actors and by audiences. What was the attitude of

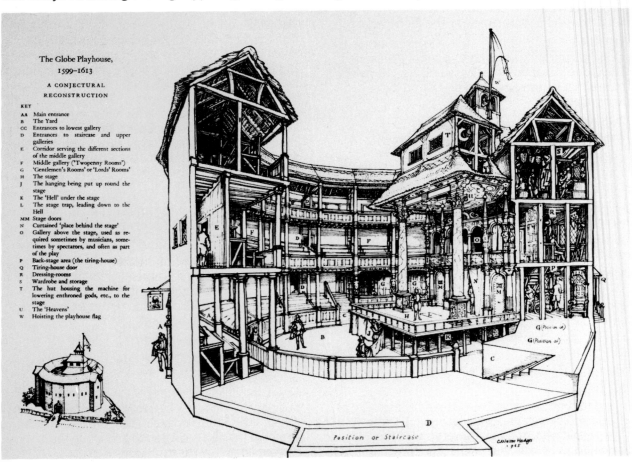

The Globe Playhouse,
1599–1613

A CONJECTURAL
RECONSTRUCTION

KEY

AA   Main entrance
B   The Yard
CC   Entrances to lowest gallery
D   Entrances to staircase and upper galleries
E   Corridor serving the different sections of the middle gallery
F   Middle gallery ('Twopenny Rooms')
G   'Gentlemen's Rooms' or 'Lords' Rooms'
H   The stage
J   The hanging being put up round the stage
K   The 'Hell' under the stage
L   The stage trap, leading down to the Hell
MM   Stage doors
N   Curtained 'place behind the stage'
O   Gallery above the stage, used as required sometimes by musicians, sometimes by spectators, and often as part of the play
P   Back-stage area (the tiring-house)
Q   Tiring-house door
R   Dressing-rooms
S   Wardrobe and storage
T   The hut housing the machine for lowering enthroned gods, etc., to the stage
U   The 'Heavens'
W   Hoisting the playhouse flag

audiences to the plays in your day?

THOMAS

Not so reverent, particularly at The Globe. You have to remember that The Globe could hold 3000 people, many of them standing all the time. The theatre wasn't a church! We didn't listen in hushed silence! We talked during the performance, some people were always coming and going. It was very informal!

INTERVIEWER

Shakespeare's plays can last up to three hours. Did you have a break during a performance to let you stretch your legs?

THOMAS

Not a break, but we could always buy some refreshment as the play went on – sausages, oranges, apples, a pot of ale. The Globe was a merry place – the old Globe, I mean, before it burned down.

INTERVIEWER

Were you in the audience when it happened?

THOMAS

Yes, I was. It was in 1613, nearly fourteen years after it had been built from the old timbers of Burbage's Theatre. The play was called 'All is True' – about Henry VIII – no, not by Shakespeare. This was another dramatist. To signal the entrance of the king, a cannon was fired. Not a cannon ball, you understand, but some paper and cloth rolled into a ball. But instead of shooting over the theatre roof, it landed in the straw thatch above the galleries. There it started to smoulder, but the audience was so taken with the play that nobody noticed the wisp of smoke rising up from the roof. Before long it had set fire to the straw and the whole theatre was ablaze. Imagine the panic! Cries and shouts of 'fire! fire!' – and everyone rushed for the exits! What was hard to believe was that no one was killed or injured, except for one man who got his breeches set on fire – and had the flames put out with a pint of ale!

INTERVIEWER

And that was the end of the famous Globe, where so many of Shakespeare's plays had seen their first productions.

THOMAS

Not quite the end. Within a year the actors had raised enough money to build a new Globe theatre, far more splendid than the first, finer than all its rivals on the South Bank.

INTERVIEWER

But by then, in 1614, there were no new plays to come from Shakespeare's pen and drama was beginning to change. For nearly four centuries it has been changing, but since your day, Thomas, there has been a thread of continuity – Shakespeare's plays. There's always at least one of his plays being performed in some theatre in London. Does it surprise you that he has remained popular for so long?

THOMAS

No. The drama of human nature doesn't change all that much: Will Shakespeare knew what would last!

INTERVIEWER

And having arrived in the twentieth century, I think we should allow you to return to the seventeenth. It wasn't such an ordeal after all, was it?

THOMAS

Not in the least. You almost persuaded me that I am a bit of an expert – and that's a great achievement!

INTERVIEWER

To us, of course, you are! Thomas Platter – thank you very much!

CHECKPOINT

Questions for written or oral answers, based on the interview with Thomas Platter.

1 At what time did performances of plays at The Globe begin?
2 What did a flying flag above the theatre indicate?
3 Why could weather affect the performance of a play at The Globe?
4 Was The Globe square, round, hexagonal or octagonal in shape?
5 Who were the 'groundlings'?
6 How many galleries were there?
7 What extra comforts did you get if you went into the galleries?
8 What was the 'tiring house'?
9 What objections did Thomas Platter have to some of the fashionable young men who went to the theatre?
10 Where did the musicians sit?
11 What kind of scenes were performed in the alcove?
12 What could the trapdoor be used for?
13 How many people could The Globe hold?
14 How did the Globe fire start?
15 When was the new Globe built?

THIS WOODEN O

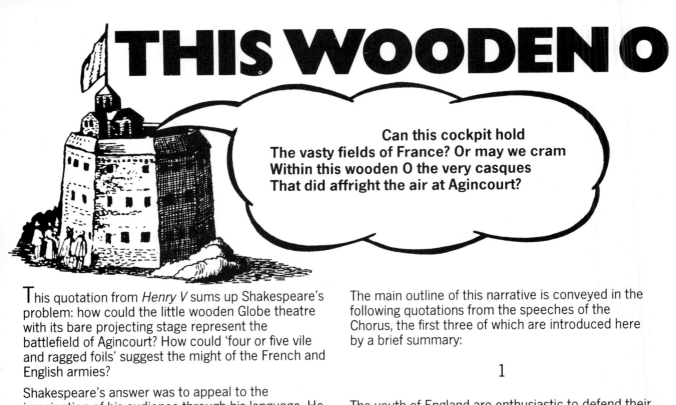

> Can this cockpit hold
> The vasty fields of France? Or may we cram
> Within this wooden O the very casques
> That did affright the air at Agincourt?

This quotation from *Henry V* sums up Shakespeare's problem: how could the little wooden Globe theatre with its bare projecting stage represent the battlefield of Agincourt? How could 'four or five vile and ragged foils' suggest the might of the French and English armies?

Shakespeare's answer was to appeal to the imagination of his audience through his language. He made them see in their mind's eye what could not be realistically presented on the stage:

Think, when we talk of horses, that you see them Printing their proud hoofs i' th' receiving earth;

In *Henry V* this role is undertaken by a figure known as the Chorus, who, at intervals throughout the play sets the scene, indicates the passage of time and narrates the events that are too great for the stage: the outbreak of war between England and France; the gathering of the English army and its setting sail for France; the siege of Harfleur, the eve of the battle of Agincourt, the triumphant return of Henry to England and his subsequent return to France to marry the princess Katherine.

The main outline of this narrative is conveyed in the following quotations from the speeches of the Chorus, the first three of which are introduced here by a brief summary:

1

The youth of England are enthusiastic to defend their country's honour and volunteer for the war.

Now all the youth of England are on fire,
And silken dalliance in the wardrobe lies;
Now thrive the armourers, and honour's thought
Reigns solely in the breast of every man;
They sell the pasture now to buy the horse,
Following the mirror of all Christian kings
With winged heels, as English Mercuries.

2

The English fleet, with the king aboard, sets sail for Harfleur.

         Suppose that you have seen
The well-appointed King at Hampton pier
Embark his royalty; and his brave fleet
With silken streamers the young Phœbus
   fanning.
Play with your fancies; and in them behold
Upon the hempen tackle ship-boys climbing;
Hear the shrill whistle which doth order give
To sounds confus'd; behold the threaden sails,
Borne with th' invisible and creeping wind,
Draw the huge bottoms through the furrowed sea,
Breasting the lofty surge. O, do but think
You stand upon the rivage and behold
A city on th' inconstant billows dancing;
For so appears this fleet majestical,
Holding due course to Harfleur. Follow, follow!

3

Every youth has joined the select army of men, leaving England to be guarded by grandfathers, babies and old women.

Grapple your minds to sternage of this navy
And leave your England as dead midnight still,
Guarded with grandsires, babies, and old women,
Either past or not arriv'd to pith and puissance;
For who is he whose chin is but enrich'd
With one appearing hair that will not follow
These cull'd and choice-drawn cavaliers to France?

To continue the story, can you write a brief summary for each of the numbered quotations?

4—8 THE EVE OF AGINCOURT

4

Work, work your thoughts, and therein see a
   siege;
Behold the ordnance on their carriages,
With fatal mouths gaping on girded Harfleur.
Suppose th' ambassador from the French comes
   back;

Tells Harry that the King doth offer him
Katharine his daughter, and with her to dowry
Some petty and unprofitable dukedoms.
The offer likes not; and the nimble gunner
With linstock now the devilish cannon touches,
            [*Alarum, and chambers go off.*
And down goes all before them. Still be kind,
And eke out our performance with your mind.

5

Now entertain conjecture of a time
When creeping murmur and the poring dark
Fills the wide vessel of the universe.
From camp to camp, through the foul womb of
   night,
The hum of either army stilly sounds,
That the fix'd sentinels almost receive
The secret whispers of each other's watch.
Fire answers fire, and through their paly flames
Each battle sees the other's umber'd face;
Steed threatens steed, in high and boastful
   neighs
Piercing the night's dull ear; and from the tents
The armourers accomplishing the knights,
With busy hammers closing rivets up,
Give dreadful note of preparation.
The country cocks do crow, the clocks do toll,
And the third hour of drowsy morning name.

6

Proud of their numbers and secure in soul,
The confident and over-lusty French
Do the low-rated English play at dice;
And chide the cripple tardy-gaited night
Who like a foul and ugly witch doth limp
So tediously away.

7

         The poor condemned English,
Like sacrifices, by their watchful fires
Sit patiently and inly ruminate
The morning's danger; and their gesture sad
Investing lank-lean cheeks, and war-worn coats,
Presenteth them unto the gazing moon
So many horrid ghosts.

8

         O, now, who will behold
The royal captain of this ruin'd band
Walking from watch to watch, from tent to tent,
Let him cry 'Praise and glory on his head!'
For forth he goes and visits all his host;
Bids them good morrow with a modest smile,
And calls them brothers, friends, and
   countrymen.

9–10 THE TRIUMPHANT RETURN TO ENGLAND

9

Now we bear the King
Toward Calais. Grant him there. There seen,
Heave him away upon your winged thoughts
Athwart the sea. Behold, the English beach
Pales in the flood with men, with wives, and boys,
Whose shouts and claps out-voice the deep-
  mouth'd sea,
Which, like a mighty whiffler, fore the King,
Seems to prepare his way. So let him land,
And solemnly see him set on to London.

10

But now behold
In the quick forge and working-house of thought,
How London doth pour out her citizens!
The mayor and all his brethren, in best sort –
Like to the senators of th' antique Rome,
With the plebeians swarming at their heels –
Go forth and fetch their conqu'ring Cæsar in:

In what way has Shakespeare helped his audience to use their imaginations?

- He has appealed directly to the audience:
  Suppose that you have seen . . .
- He has given them vivid word-pictures:
  Upon the hempen tackle ship-boys climbing
- He has emphasised the sounds that would be heard in the scene:
  Hear the shrill whistle which doth order give
  To sounds confus'd
- He has used figures of speech such as metaphor, simile and personification:
  A city on th' inconstant billows dancing

Now look over the quotations again and find four more examples for each of these categories which, in your opinion, illustrate the way Shakespeare, through language, overcame the limitations of 'the wooden O'.

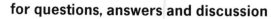

FORUM

for questions, answers and discussion

When Shakespeare wrote his history plays, did he stick strictly to historical fact, or did he change things to make his plays more interesting and dramatic?

He changed things. He took his English history from an historian called Holinshed and his Roman history from a writer called Plutarch whose works had been translated into English. But you can't telescope years and years of history into a three-hour play without distorting something.

Besides, Shakespeare had to produce characters that would interest and excite his audience — not just historical cardboard cut-outs. He gave Richard III a hump on his back, a limp, a long nose and made him murder the princes in the Tower; but there's no historical proof that Richard was either deformed or a child-murderer. He also makes Henry V a more romantic figure than he was in real life — part fact, part fiction.

Similarly, Cleopatra was an historical figure and her relationship with Antony is the basis of Shakespeare's play — but her character is almost one hundred percent the creation of Shakespeare's imagination!

● Does it matter that Shakespeare altered history — or that he recreated historical characters for his own purposes?

● What is the loss? What is the gain?

● What historical characters have you seen portrayed on television or on film? Are they likely to be closer to the truth than Shakespeare's characters were?

SOLILOQUIES

In Shakespeare's plays you will almost certainly come across a speech known as a 'soliloquy'. The character will be 'thinking aloud', letting the audience overhear his thoughts. It is a dramatic device used to give the audience information or to reveal motives and intentions that are not revealed to other characters. The tragedies, in particular, contain some very fine soliloquies which take the spectator or the reader into the very heart of the characters who speak them. Here are two examples of soliloquies: the first is from *Romeo and Juliet*, the second from *Richard III*.

JULIET'S FEARS

Romeo has been banished from Verona for killing Tybalt (Juliet's cousin) in a duel, but before leaving he has secretly married Juliet. Her parents, however, are insisting that she marries Paris, an aristocratic suitor. To avoid the marriage, Juliet agrees to take a special potion, concocted by Friar Lawrence, which will have the effect of making her appear dead. She will be buried in the family vault, but within forty-two hours the effects of the potion will have worn off and she will be restored to life — and Romeo. In this dramatic soliloquy Juliet reveals her doubts and fears before she drinks the potion.

JULIET

[Exeunt Lady Capulet and Nurse.

Farewell! God knows when we shall meet again.
I have a faint cold fear thrills through my veins,
That almost freezes up the heat of life;
I'll call them back again to comfort me.
Nurse! – What should she do here?
My dismal scene I needs must act alone.
Come, vial.
What if this mixture do not work at all?
Shall I be married, then, to-morrow morning?
No, no; this shall forbid it. Lie thou there.
[Laying down her dagger.
What if it be a poison which the friar
Subtly hath minist'red to have me dead,
Lest in this marriage he should be dishonour'd,
Because he married me before to Romeo?
I fear it is; and yet methinks it should not,
For he hath still been tried a holy man.
How if, when I am laid into the tomb,
I wake before the time that Romeo
Come to redeem me? There's a fearful point.
Shall I not then be stifled in the vault,
To whose foul mouth no healthsome air breathes
    in,
And there die strangled ere my Romeo comes?
Or, if I live, is it not very like
The horrible conceit of death and night,
Together with the terror of the place –
As in a vault, an ancient receptacle
Where for this many hundred years the bones
Of all my buried ancestors are pack'd;
Where bloody Tybalt, yet but green in earth,
Lies fest'ring in his shroud; where, as they say,
At some hours in the night spirits resort –
Alack, alack, is it not like that I,
So early waking – what with loathsome smells,
And shrieks like mandrakes' torn out of the earth,
That living mortals, hearing them, run mad –
O, if I wake, shall I not be distraught,
Environed with all these hideous fears,
And madly play with my forefathers' joints,
And pluck the mangled Tybalt from his shroud,
And, in this rage, with some great kinsman's bone,
As with a club, dash out my desp'rate brains?
O, look! methinks I see my cousin's ghost
Seeking out Romeo, that did spit his body
Upon a rapier's point. Stay, Tybalt, stay.
Romeo, I come. This do I drink to thee.
[She drinks and falls upon her bed within
the curtains.

Romeo and Juliet, Act 4, Scene 3

RICHARD'S WOOING

Lady Anne is accompanying the corpse of King
Henry VI to its burial place when the procession is
interrupted by Richard, Duke of Gloucester – the self-
confessed murderer, not only of the king, but also of
Lady Anne's husband, Edward. He protests that the
murders were done for love of her and pleads with
her to marry him. At first she scorns this 'lump of foul

deformity', but eventually softens and leaves him with
some hope of being accepted. It is then that Richard
limps downstage to confide in the audience.

RICHARD

Was ever woman in this humour woo'd?
Was ever woman in this humour won?
I'll have her; but I will not keep her long.
What! I that kill'd her husband and his father –
To take her in her heart's extremest hate,
With curses in her mouth, tears in her eyes,
The bleeding witness of my hatred by;
Having God, her conscience, and these bars
    against me,
And I no friends to back my suit at all
But the plain devil and dissembling looks,
And yet to win her, all the world to nothing!
Ha!
Hath she forgot already that brave prince,
Edward, her lord, whom I, some three months
    since,
Stabb'd in my angry mood at Tewksbury?
A sweeter and a lovelier gentleman –
Fram'd in the prodigality of nature,
Young, valiant, wise, and no doubt right royal –
The spacious world cannot again afford;
And will she yet abase her eyes on me,
That cropp'd the golden prime of this sweet prince
And made her widow to a woeful bed?
On me, whose all not equals Edward's moiety?
On me, that halts and am misshapen thus?
My dukedom to a beggarly denier,
I do mistake my person all this while.
Upon my life, she finds, although I cannot,
Myself to be a marv'llous proper man.
I'll be at charges for a looking-glass,
And entertain a score or two of tailors
To study fashions to adorn my body.
Since I am crept in favour with myself,
I will maintain it with some little cost.
But first I'll turn yon fellow in his grave,
And then return lamenting to my love.
Shine out, fair sun, till I have bought a glass,
That I may see my shadow as I pass

King Richard III, Act 1, Scene 2

(?) Both Juliet and Richard reveal to the
audience what they would not reveal to
another character in the play.
Why is it necessary that Juliet's speech is a soliloquy?
What thoughts does Richard share with the audience
that he would conceal from Lady Anne?

(?) Can you express in your own words some of
Juliet's fears?

(?) Which, in your opinion, are the most
dramatic lines of her soliloquy?
If you were in a theatre, listening to Richard's
soliloquy, what do you think your reaction would be?
At what point in the speech would you feel most
strongly against him?
Where would you sympathise? Would you be amused?

<h1 style="text-align:center">The most lamentable comedy and most cruel
death of Pyramus and Thisby from</h1>

A MIDSUMMER NIGHT'S DREAM

This extract comes from the end of the play when all the complications of the plot have been unravelled.

It is the wedding night of DUKE THESEUS OF ATHENS and HIPPOLYTA, QUEEN OF THE AMAZONS. To celebrate the nuptials, a play is presented to the court – not by a polished, professional troupe, but by a small group of amateur enthusiasts, who in their daily lives are simple craftsmen.

Their play is entitled 'The most lamentable comedy, and most cruel death of Pyramus and Thisby'. It brings forth dry, critical but amused comments from the courtly spectators, but the larger audience in the theatre itself is usually delighted by the craftsmen's comic attempts to present a tragedy.

To read or act the scene, you will need:

PHILOSTRATE Master of the Revels
THESEUS Duke of Athens
HIPPOLYTA Queen of the Amazons
DEMETRIUS a young Athenian
LYSANDER a young Athenian
PETER QUINCE, a carpenter who acts THE PROLOGUE
NICK BOTTOM, a weaver who acts PYRAMUS
FRANCIS FLUTE, a bellows-mender who acts THISBY
TOM SNOUT, a tinker who acts WALL
ROBIN STARVELING, a tailor who acts MOONSHINE
SNUG, a joiner who acts LION

Your reading or acting will be greatly improved if you write some production notes first!

ACT 5, SCENE 1

Re-enter PHILOSTRATE.

PHILOSTRATE	So please your Grace, the Prologue is address'd.
THESEUS	Let him approach. [*Flourish of trumpets.*

Enter QUINCE *as the* PROLOGUE.

PROLOGUE	*If we offend, it is with our good will.*
	That you should think, we come not to offend,
	But with good will. To show our simple skill, 110
	That is the true beginning of our end.
	Consider then, we come but in despite.
	We do not come, as minding to content you,
	Our true intent is. All for your delight
	We are not here. That you should here repent you, 115
	The actors are at hand; and, by their show,
	You shall know all, that you are like to know.
THESEUS	This fellow doth not stand upon points.
LYSANDER	He hath rid his prologue like a rough colt; he knows
	not the stop. A good moral, my lord: it is not enough to 120
	speak, but to speak true.
HIPPOLYTA	Indeed he hath play'd on this prologue like a child on
	a recorder – a sound, but not in government.
THESEUS	His speech was like a tangled chain; nothing
	impaired, but all disordered. Who is next? 125

123 *government*: control

Enter, with a TRUMPET *, as in dumb
show,* PYRAMUS *and* THISBY, WALL, MOONSHINE,
and LION.

PROLOGUE	*Gentles, perchance you wonder at this show;*
	But wonder on, till truth make all things plain.
	This man is Pyramus, if you would know;

This beauteous lady Thisby is certain.
This man, with lime and rough-cast, doth present 130
Wall, that vile Wall which did these lovers sunder;
And through Wall's chink, poor souls, they are content
To whisper. At the which let no man wonder.
This man, with lanthorn, dog, and bush of thorn,
Presenteth Moonshine; for, if you will know, 135
By moonshine did these lovers think no scorn
To meet at Ninus' tomb, there, there to woo.
This grisly beast, which Lion hight by name,   138 *hight*: is called
The trusty Thisby, coming first by night,
Did scare away, or rather did affright; 140
And as she fled, her mantle she did fall;   141 *mantle*: cloak
Which Lion vile with bloody mouth did stain.
Anon comes Pyramus, sweet youth and tall,
And finds his trusty Thisby's mantle slain;
Whereat with blade, with bloody blameful blade, 145
He bravely broach'd his boiling bloody breast;   146 *broach'd*: pierced
And Thisby, tarrying in mulberry shade,
His dagger drew, and died. For all the rest,
Let Lion, Moonshine, Wall, and lovers twain,
At large discourse while here they do remain. 150   150 *at large discourse*:
      Exeunt Prologue, Pyramus, Thisby, Lion, and   speak more fully
      Moonshine.

THESEUS   I wonder if the lion be to speak.

DEMETRIUS   No wonder, my lord: one lion may, when many asses do.

WALL   *In this same interlude it doth befall*   153 *interlude*: short
That I, one Snout by name, present a wall;   play
And such a wall as I would have you think 155
That had in it a crannied hole or chink,
Through which the lovers, Pyramus and Thisby,
Did whisper often very secretly.
This loam, this rough-cast, and this stone, doth show
That I am that same wall; the truth is so; 160
And this the cranny is, right and sinister,
Through which the fearful lovers are to whisper.

THESEUS	Would you desire lime and hair to speak better?
DEMETRIUS	It is the wittiest partition that ever I heard discourse, my lord. 165

Enter PYRAMUS.

THESEUS	Pyramus draws near the wall; silence.
PYRAMUS	*O grim-look'd night! O night with hue so black!*
	O night, which ever art when day is not!
	O night, O night, alack, alack, alack,
	I fear my Thisby's promise is forgot! 170
	And thou, O wall, O sweet, O lovely wall,
	That stand'st between her father's ground and mine;
	Thou wall, O wall, O sweet and lovely wall,
	Show me thy chink, to blink through with mine eyne.
	[Wall holds up his fingers.
	Thanks, courteous wall. Jove shield thee well for this! 175
	But what see I? No Thisby do I see.
	O wicked wall, through whom I see no bliss;
	Curs'd be thy stones for thus deceiving me!
THESEUS	The wall, methinks, being sensible, should curse again.
PYRAMUS	No, in truth, sir, he should not. *Deceiving me* is 180 Thisby's cue. She is to enter now, and I am to spy her through the wall. You shall see it will fall pat as I told you; yonder she comes.

179 *sensible*: able to use its senses (i.e. talk)

Enter THISBY.

THISBY	*O wall, full often hast thou heard my moans,*
	For parting my fair Pyramus and me! 185
	My cherry lips have often kiss'd thy stones,
	Thy stones with lime and hair knit up in thee.
PYRAMUS	*I see a voice; now will I to the chink,*
	To spy an I can hear my Thisby's face.
	Thisby! 190
THISBY	*My love! thou art my love, I think.*
PYRAMUS	*Think what thou wilt, I am thy lover's grace;*
	And like Limander am I trusty still.
THISBY	*And I like Helen, till the Fates me kill.*
PYRAMUS	*Not Shafalus to Procrus was so true.* 195
THISBY	*As Shafalus to Procrus, I to you.*
PYRAMUS	*O, kiss me through the hole of this vile wall.*
THISBY	*I kiss the wall's hole, not your lips at all.*
PYRAMUS	*Wilt thou at Ninny's tomb meet me straightway?*
THISBY	*Tide life, tide death, I come without delay.* 200
	[Exeunt Pyramus and Thisby.
WALL	*Thus have I, Wall, my part discharged so;*
	And, being done, thus Wall away doth go. *[Exit Wall.*
THESEUS	Now is the moon used between the two neighbours.
DEMETRIUS	No remedy, my lord, when walls are so wilful to hear without warning. 205
HIPPOLYTA	This is the silliest stuff that ever I heard.
THESEUS	The best in this kind are but shadows; and the worst are no worse, if imagination amend them.
HIPPOLYTA	It must be your imagination then, and not theirs.
THESEUS	If we imagine no worse of them than they of themselves, 210 they may pass for excellent men. Here come two noble beasts in, a man and a lion.

193–6 Famous lovers: *Limander* = Leander, *Helen* = Helen of Troy, *Shafalus* = Cephalus, *Procrus* = Procis

200 *Tide*: come

Enter LION and MOONSHINE.

44

LION	*You, ladies, you, whose gentle hearts do fear*
	The smallest monstrous mouse that creeps on floor,
	May now, perchance, both quake and tremble here, 215
	When lion rough in wildest rage doth roar.
	Then know that I as Snug the joiner am
	A lion fell, nor else no lion's dam;
	For, if I should as lion come in strife
	Into this place, 'twere pity on my life. 220
THESEUS	A very gentle beast, and of a good conscience.
DEMETRIUS	The very best at a beast, my lord, that e'er I saw.
LYSANDER	This lion is a very fox for his valour.
THESEUS	True; and a goose for his discretion.
DEMETRIUS	Not so, my lord; for his valour cannot carry his 225
	discretion, and the fox carries the goose.
THESEUS	His discretion, I am sure, cannot carry his valour;
	for the goose carries not the fox. It is well. Leave it to his
	discretion, and let us listen to the Moon.
MOON	*This lanthorn doth the horned moon present —* 230
DEMETRIUS	He should have worn the horns on his head.
THESEUS	He is no crescent, and his horns are invisible within
	the circumference.
MOON	*This lanthorn doth the horned moon present;*
	Myself the Man i' the th' Moon do seem to be. 235
THESEUS	This is the greatest error of all the rest; the man
	should be put into the lantern. How is it else the man i'
	th' moon?
DEMETRIUS	He dares not come there for the candle; for, you
	see, it is already in snuff. 240
HIPPOLYTA	I am aweary of this moon. Would he would change!
THESEUS	It appears, by his small light of discretion, that he is
	in the wane; but yet, in courtesy, in all reason, we must
	stay the time.
LYSANDER	Proceed, Moon. 245
MOON	All that I have to say is to tell you that the lanthorn
	is the moon; I, the Man i' the Moon; this thorn-bush, my
	thorn-bush; and this dog, my dog.
DEMETRIUS	Why, all these should be in the lantern; for all these
	are in the moon. But silence; here comes Thisby. 250
	Re-enter THISBY.
THISBY	*This is old Ninny's tomb. Where is my love?*
LION	*[Roaring.]* O — *[Thisby runs off.*
DEMETRIUS	Well roar'd, Lion.
THESEUS	Well run, Thisby.
HIPPOLYTA	Well shone, Moon. Truly, the moon shines with a 255
	good grace. *[The Lion tears Thisby's mantle, and exit.*
THESEUS	Well mous'd, Lion.
	Re-enter PYRAMUS.
DEMETRIUS	And then came Pyramus.
LYSANDER	And so the lion vanish'd.
PYRAMUS	*Sweet Moon, I thank thee for thy sunny beams;* 260
	I thank thee, Moon, for shining now so bright;
	For, by thy gracious, golden, glittering gleams,
	I trust to take of truest Thisby sight.
	But stay, O spite!
	But mark, poor knight, 265
	What dreadful dole is here!
	Eyes, do you see?

218 *fell*: skin

239 *for the candle*: because the candle is already in the lantern

240 *in snuff*: annoyed

266 *dole*: grief

45

         How can it be?
    O dainty duck! O dear!
      Thy mantle good,   270
    What! stain'd with blood?
    Approach, ye Furies fell.
      O Fates! come, come;   274 *Cut thread and*
      Cut thread and thrum;   *thrum*: cut the
    Quail, crush, conclude, and quell.   275 thread of life

THESEUS   This passion, and the death of a dear friend, would go   275 *quail*: to
near to make a man look sad.   overpower

HIPPOLYTA   Beshrew my heart, but I pity the man.

PYRAMUS   *O wherefore, Nature, didst thou lions frame?*
Since lion vile hath here deflower'd my dear;   280 280 *deflower'd*:
Which is – no, no – which was the fairest dame   Bottom means
That liv'd, that lov'd, that lik'd, that look'd with cheer.   'devoured'
    Come, tears confound;   283 *confound*: flow,
    Out, sword, and wound   pour out
    The pap of Pyramus;   285 285 *pap*: breast
      Ay, that left pap,
      Where heart doth hop.   *[Stabs himself.*
    Thus die I, thus, thus, thus.
      Now am I dead,
      Now am I fled;   290
    My soul is in the sky.
      Tongue, lose thy light;
      Moon, take thy flight.   *[Exit Moonshine.*
    Now die, die, die, die, die.   *[Dies.*

DEMETRIUS   No die, but an ace, for him; for he is but one.   295 295 *die*: a pun. It also
                        means 'dice'

LYSANDER   Less than an ace, man; for he is dead; he is nothing.   295 *ace*: a pun. It also

THESEUS   With the help of a surgeon he might yet recover and   means 'ass'
yet prove an ass.

HIPPOLYTA   How chance Moonshine is gone before Thisby comes
back and finds her lover?   300

               Re-enter THISBY.

THESEUS   She will find him by starlight. Here she comes; and
her passion ends the play.

HIPPOLYTA   Methinks she should not use a long one for such a
Pyramus; I hope she will be brief.

DEMETRIUS   A mote will turn the balance, which Pyramus, which   305 305 *mote*: speck of
Thisby is the better – he for a man, God warrant us: she   dust
for a woman, God bless us!

LYSANDER   She hath spied him already with those sweet eyes.

DEMETRIUS   And thus she moans, videlicet: –   309 *moans*: laments
                       309 *videlicet*: a legal

THISBY   *Asleep, my love?*   310   term meaning
    What, dead, my dove?   'namely'
    O Pyramus, arise,
      Speak, speak. Quite dumb?
      Dead, dead? A tomb
    Must cover thy sweet eyes.   315
      These lily lips,
      This cherry nose,
    These yellow cowslip cheeks,
      Are gone, are gone;
      Lovers, make moan;   320
    His eyes were green as leeks.
      O Sisters Three,
      Come, come to me,
    With hands as pale as milk;
      Lay them in gore,   325
      Since you have shore   326 *shore*: cut

With shears his thread of silk.
Tongue, not a word.
Come, trusty sword;
Come, blade, my breast imbrue. [*Stabs herself.*   330
And farewell, friends;
Thus Thisby ends;
Adieu, adieu, adieu.   [*Dies.*

THESEUS   Moonshine and Lion are left to bury the dead.

DEMETRIUS   Ay, and Wall too.   335

BOTTOM   [*Starting up.*] No, I assure you; the wall is down
that parted their fathers. Will it please you to see the
Epilogue, or to hear a Bergomask dance between two of
our company?

THESEUS   No epilogue, I pray you; for your play needs no excuse.   340
Never excuse; for when the players are all dead there
need none to be blamed. Marry, if he that writ it had
played Pyramus, and hang'd himself in Thisby's garter,
it would have been a fine tragedy. And so it is, truly; and
very notably discharg'd. But come, your Bergomask; let   345
your epilogue alone.   [*A dance.*
The iron tongue of midnight hath told twelve.
Lovers, to bed; 'tis almost fairy time.
I fear we shall out-sleep the coming morn,
As much as we this night have overwatch'd.   350
This palpable-gross play hath well beguil'd
The heavy gait of night. Sweet friends, to bed,
A fortnight hold we this solemnity,
In nightly revels and new jollity.   [*Exeunt.*

---

330 *imbrue*: stain with blood

338 *epilogue*: a speech to end the play (opposite of the prologue)

342 *Marry*: by Mary!

Hippolyta calls it 'the silliest stuff that ever I heard' — and, indeed, it is; but performed by good actors, it is also the funniest.

The comedy depends on many things, but particularly on the language — its clever use and its misuse, though the verbal jokes are often missed at a first reading. Look over the scene again and try to identify some of these tricks:

✱ Quince's confused punctuation, such as his opening remark: 'If we offend it is with our good will.'

✱ Bottom's misuse of words;

✱ the confusion of verbs, especially 'see' and 'hear';

✱ alliteration that is comically exaggerated;

✱ the puns of the courtly characters;

✱ — and any other examples of verbal humour that have struck you.

An Interview with NATHAN

PRESENTER

Thomas Platter gave us the spectator's view of the Elizabethan stage; Richard Burbage gave us the star performer's. Our next interview is with one of the younger actors in Shakespeare's company — one of the boy apprentices who learnt the art of acting from the older members and perhaps from Shakespeare himself. His name is Nathan.

INTERVIEWER

Hello, Nathan. We know that you were a member of the Lord Chamberlain's Men, later to become the King's Men. How old were you when you joined the company?

NATHAN

I must have been about eleven.

INTERVIEWER

And how long were you in the company as one of its junior members?

NATHAN

Until my voice broke and I began to grow a beard! I began as an apprentice and, like all apprentices, I had to learn my craft from those who had already mastered it.

INTERVIEWER

And who better than Richard Burbage?

NATHAN

Yes, Dick, but also Will Shakespeare. He often directed us in our parts and because he had written the plays he knew exactly how he wanted them performed.

INTERVIEWER

Can you tell us something of the approach he had to acting? Did he ever lose his temper and storm out of the theatre because you were ruining his lines?

NATHAN

No, not quite, but certain types of acting used to annoy him. You have read *Hamlet*, I suppose? (The Interviewer nods.) Then you know the advice that Hamlet gives to the players who are visiting the royal court:

'Speak the speech, I pray you, as I pronounc'd it to you, trippingly on the tongue; but if you mouth it, as many of our players do, I had as lief the town-crier spoke my lines.'

That was Will speaking to us. He hated an actor who 'strutted and bellowed' — one who would 'tear a passion to tatters, to very rags, to split the ears of the groundlings'. Then there were the comedians who departed from the script and held up the plot while they did their own comic business — he couldn't bear them either!

INTERVIEWER

As he had every right to! He presumably wanted the actor to submerge himself in the part and not play to the gallery!

66 boys played all the women's parts 99

NATHAN

It was playing to the groundlings that was the trouble, not playing to the galleries!

INTERVIEWER

Of course! But as you were a small company, Shakespeare must have had individual actors in mind when he was writing his plays — Burbage for Shylock and Lear, for example. He could write parts for their particular talents. Did he create any roles specially for the young actors?

NATHAN

We apprentices used to have all the small parts, you know — pigmies, fairies, beggars, page boys and young children. And boys played all the women's parts too – that's why there are so few female characters in the plays. I stopped being a boy actor when my voice broke and I grew a beard!

INTERVIEWER
Why weren't the female roles taken by women?

NATHAN
It wasn't considered respectable for women to act in public theatres. Even the male actors were thought of as rogues and vagabonds by some of the City authorities – that's why most of the theatres were outside the City boundaries.

INTERVIEWER
Wasn't it difficult getting the audience to take you seriously as women?
Didn't they laugh and scoff?

NATHAN
Not at all. Boy players were very popular with playgoers. In wigs and dresses we were very convincing as women. Besides, Will often made it easier for us by developing plots in which the girls dress up as boys to conceal their real identity – *Twelfth Night*, *As You Like It*, *The Merchant of Venice*, *Cymbeline* –

INTERVIEWER
So the great roles of Juliet and Cleopatra were originally played by boys?

NATHAN
Yes.

INTERVIEWER
And you, Nathan? Which of the great female roles fell to you?

NATHAN
Well as you can see, I'm rather tall and thin. Do you remember that in *A Midsummer Night's Dream* Helena is described as being like 'a painted maypole'? I was Helena. And in *As You Like It* Rosalind speaks of herself as 'more than common tall'? I was Rosalind.

INTERVIEWER
These are very demanding parts for a young boy to play in a professional theatre. The young actors in your day obviously had to be very talented.

NATHAN
With a different play to perform each day, we had to be on our toes! But the apprentices didn't only act. We were general dogsbodies! We were at everyone's beck and call – sent to the tailor to collect the costumes, put in charge of properties, sent out to buy the ale, told to make sure that the cannon was prepared – there were a hundred and one jobs to do as well as act! And when we were touring it was even more hectic!

INTERVIEWER
We know that the theatres in London closed during the plague years and that acting companies took themselves off to the provinces with their repertory of plays. Were you glad to get away from London?

NATHAN
It was hard work, travelling those long, dusty roads with our horse-drawn carts loaded up with our costumes, spears, swords, crowns, beards, wigs and wooden pies. After the glories of our royal performances we were strolling players once more, roughing it!

INTERVIEWER
Much more comfortable to have remained in town! Had you ever considered leaving the public theatre and joining one of the private companies of boy actors?

NATHAN
No, I had more scope in Shakespeare's company than I would have had anywhere else, but boy actors were in great demand to play the female roles and could be bought and sold like merchandise by the actor managers.

66 We were general dogsbodies 99

INTERVIEWER
A little like top football players in the twentieth century! Was there great rivalry amongst the companies to get the best writers and actors?

NATHAN
Yes, and particularly between the adult companies and the companies of boy actors, who performed in the private theatres which were *inside* the City limits and therefore considered more respectable! There were two main companies, one from the choir of St Paul's Cathedral and the other from the choir of the Chapel Royal. Their singing and dancing and delicate playing attracted a better kind of audience than we did in our rather rough and ready theatre and for a time they quite overshadowed us. But there was the problem of continually having to replace boys whose voices broke, whereas we kept the same players for years and years.

INTERVIEWER
And when your days as a boy actor were over, what happened? Did you stay on to play important male roles and leave Helena and Rosalind to your younger successor?

NATHAN
Yes. Then I too became a kind of master and taught apprentices to act, just as I had been taught: and so the profession continued and grew and the tradition of art was preserved. I hope some of it has found its way to the twentieth century.

INTERVIEWER
I'm sure it has; and if you were to see our Shakespeare productions, perhaps you would recognise some of the technique. Only now Juliet, Cleopatra and Portia would be played by women, not by boys.

NATHAN
By women? They're not ashamed to be seen on the public stage?

INTERVIEWER
No, they're proud of it! Many a girl dreams of being a famous actress performing before an admiring audience.

NATHAN
And the boys? What parts do they play now?

INTERVIEWER
They usually play boys' parts, I'm afraid. The young Nathan of today has to be content with less spectacular parts than you played. He wouldn't start his career as an apprentice to a great actor in a theatrical company, but as a student in a drama school.

NATHAN
Yet filled with the same love of acting, struggling to interpret the lines and create a living character from them?

INTERVIEWER
I think so.

NATHAN
Then things haven't changed so much! We belong to the same profession! Thank you for reassuring me!

INTERVIEWER
Thank you, Nathan.

WRITE A STORY OR A DIARY based on the life of a boy-actor in the Elizabethan theatre. Read over the interviews with Burbage, Thomas Platter and Nathan to gather some background material and consult the list of books on p. 70, but don't be afraid to use your imagination to fill out the bare facts. Concentrate on a single day, or span a wider period to take in touring — and introduce Shakespeare as a character if you wish.

Blank Verse

If you look at a typical speech from a Shakespearean play, you will see that it is set out like this:

Say that she rail; why, then I'll tell her plain
She sings as sweetly as a nightingale.
Say that she frown; I'll say she looks as clear
As morning roses newly wash'd with dew.

The lines are roughly the same length, but they do not cover the width of the page, as they would if they were written in prose. They are, in fact, written in verse form and each line contains exactly ten syllables. Count them.

The ten syllables can be divided into five that are stressed (\) and five that are unstressed (ᴗ), alternating with each other:

Sӑy thȁt shĕ rȁil; whӗy, thȅn I̎ll tȅll hĕr plȁin
Shĕ sȋngs ăs sweetlӗ as ӑ nȋghtȋngȁle;
Sӑy thȁt shĕ frȍwn; I̎ll sȁy shĕ lȍoks ӑs clȅar
Ăs mȍrnȋng rȍsĕs nȅwlӗ wȁsh'd ᴗith dȅw.

The length of a line of verse, measured by counting the stresses, is called the METRE.

When there are five stresses, the line is called a PENTAMETER.

When the lines do not rhyme, however, they are said to be BLANK.

Most of Shakespeare's plays are written in BLANK VERSE and the metre he uses is PENTAMETER.

All this sounds very technical and if Shakespeare stuck rigidly to blank verse throughout his plays he would become rather monotonous; but he manages to avoid monotony, not only by writing some speeches and scenes in prose, but by introducing variations in the blank verse itself. This is what he does:

- Instead of introducing a pause at the end of each line (through the use of a comma, full-stop or semi-colon), he runs one line into the next (called 'enjambment') and the listener is not so aware of the five-stress pattern.

- He introduces pauses in the middle of a line to break up the pentameter, sometimes dividing a line between two different speakers.

- He occasionally drops the ten-syllable line altogether.

In addition to Shakespeare's variations, there are the changes of pattern that can be brought about by the actor's interpretation of the lines. Only a very bad actor would deliver them in such a way that the listeners would be conscious of the pentameters.

Remember that the -ed at the end of a word was pronounced as a separate syllable. Thus, *vexed* counted as two syllables, but *vex'd* as one. Shakespeare would choose between the 'd and the -ed ending according to the number of syllables he wanted in a line:
Hugg'd and embraced by the strumpet wind
would be a ten-syllable line.

1

The lovers' entanglements in *A Midsummer Night's Dream* are too complicated to summarize briefly, but to understand the following passage, all you need to know is that Lysander *was* in love with Hermia (who is small), but, owing to a trick that has been played on him, he now loves Helena (who is very tall). Hermia blames Helena for stealing Lysander's affections — and thinks she did it all by her height!

HERMIA	What! Can you do me greater harm than hate?	
	Hate me! wherefore? O me! what news, my love?	272 *what news*: what does this mean?
	Am not I Hermia? Are not you Lysander?	
	I am as fair now as I was erewhile.	274 *erewhile*: previously
	Since night you lov'd me; yet since night you left me. 275	
	Why then, you left me – O, the gods forbid! –	
	In earnest, shall I say?	
LYSANDER	Ay, by my life!	
	And never did desire to see thee more.	
	Therefore be out of hope, of question, of doubt; 280	
	Be certain, nothing truer; 'tis no jest	
	That I do hate thee and love Helena.	
HERMIA	O me! you juggler! you canker-blossom!	283 *juggler*: deceiver
	You thief of love! What! Have you come by night,	283 *canker-blossom*: a maggot in a rose bud
	And stol'n my love's heart from him? 285	
HELENA	Fine, i' faith!	
	Have you no modesty, no maiden shame,	
	No touch of bashfulness? What! Will you tear	
	Impatient answers from my gentle tongue?	
	Fie, fie! you counterfeit, you puppet you! 290	
HERMIA	'Puppet'! why so? Ay, that way goes the game.	
	Now I perceive that she hath made compare	
	Between our statures; she hath urg'd her height;	
	And with her personage, her tall personage,	
	Her height, forsooth, she hath prevail'd with him. 295	
	And are you grown so high in his esteem	
	Because I am so dwarfish and so low?	
	How low am I, thou painted maypole? Speak.	
	How low am I? I am not yet so low,	
	But that my nails can reach unto thine eyes. 300	

A Midsummer Night's Dream, Act 3, Scene 2

Clarence, (whom we shall meet again later in this book) has been imprisoned in the Tower by his ambitious brother, Richard, Duke of Gloucester. He tells the Keeper that he has passed a miserable night, full of 'fearful dreams and ugly sights'.

KEEPER	What was your dream, my lord? I pray you tell me.
CLARENCE	Methoughts that I had broken from the Tower
	And was embark'd to cross to Burgundy;
	And in my company my brother Gloucester,
	Who from my cabin tempted me to walk
	Upon the hatches. Thence we look'd toward England,
	And cited up a thousand heavy times,
	During the wars of York and Lancaster,
	That had befall'n us. As we pac'd along
	Upon the giddy footing of the hatches,
	Methought that Gloucester stumbled, and in falling
	Struck me, that thought to stay him, overboard
	Into the tumbling billows of the main.
	O Lord, methought what pain it was to drown,
	What dreadful noise of waters in my ears,
	What sights of ugly death within my eyes!
	Methoughts I saw a thousand fearful wrecks,
	A thousand men that fishes gnaw'd upon,
	Wedges of gold, great anchors, heaps of pearl,
	Inestimable stones, unvalued jewels,
	All scatt'red in the bottom of the sea;
	Some lay in dead men's skulls, and in the holes
	Where eyes did once inhabit there were crept,
	As 'twere in scorn of eyes, reflecting gems,
	That woo'd the slimy bottom of the deep
	And mock'd the dead bones that lay scatt'red by.

Richard III, Act 1, Scene 4

1 From either of the two extracts, point out one example of each of the following:

  a run-on lines (or enjambment);
  b regular end-stopped pentameter;
  c a single pause in the middle of a line;
  d several pauses in a single line;
  e a line containing more than ten syllables;
  f a line containing less than ten syllables;
  g pentameter split between two speakers.

2 Which of the two extracts is more recognisable as blank verse?
   Can you suggest a reason?

3 Look carefully at the punctuation in the two extracts – particularly noting where full-stops and question marks occur. Now read or act the speeches, bringing out the feelings of the characters by varying your pace and expression, but at the same time trying to keep something of the rhythmical flow of the blank verse.

A scene from *Twelfth Night*

We shall read this scene, first from the point of view of Orsino, Duke of Illyria, then from the point of view of the audience and study the dramatic difference.

Orsino has recently taken into his court a youth named Cesario, whom he has employed in carrying messages of love to the Countess Olivia on his behalf. Olivia has rejected all the proposals, but Orsino's love is so passionate he will not accept a refusal and bids Cesario return to Olivia. Before he goes, however, Cesario poses a question: if a woman loved Orsino with the passion he has for Olivia, yet Orsino didn't love her, would *she* have to be satisfied with a rejection?

ACT 2, SCENE 4

DUKE	Once more, Cesario,		
	Get thee to yond same sovereign cruelty.	80	80 *sovereign cruelty*: i.e. Olivia
	Tell her my love, more noble than the world,		
	Prizes not quantity of dirty lands;		
	The parts that fortune hath bestow'd upon her,		
	Tell her I hold as giddily as Fortune;		84 *giddily*: carelessly
	But 'tis that miracle and queen of gems	85	
	That Nature pranks her in attracts my soul.		86 *pranks*: adorns
CESARIO	But if she cannot love you, sir?		
DUKE	I cannot be so answer'd.		
CESARIO	Sooth, but you must.		
	Say that some lady, as perhaps there is,	90	
	Hath for your love as great a pang of heart		
	As you have for Olivia. You cannot love her;		
	You tell her so. Must she not then be answer'd?		
DUKE	There is no woman's sides		
	Can bide the beating of so strong a passion	95	
	As love doth give my heart; no woman's heart		
	So big to hold so much; they lack retention.		
	Alas, their love may be call'd appetite –		
	No motion of the liver, but the palate –		
	That suffer surfeit, cloyment, and revolt;	100	
	But mine is all as hungry as the sea,		
	And can digest as much. Make no compare		
	Between that love a woman can bear me		
	And that I owe Olivia.		
CESARIO	Ay, but I know –	105	
DUKE	What dost thou know?		
CESARIO	Too well what love women to men may owe.		
	In faith, they are as true of heart as we.		
	My father had a daughter lov'd a man,		
	As it might be perhaps, were I a woman,	110	

	I should your lordship.		
DUKE	And what's her history?		
CESARIO	A blank, my lord. She never told her love,		
	But let concealment, like a worm i' th' bud,		
	Feed on her damask cheek. She pin'd in thought;	115	115 *damask*: red and white
	And with a green and yellow melancholy		
	She sat like Patience on a monument,		
	Smiling at grief. Was not this love indeed?		
	We men may say more, swear more, but indeed		
	Our shows are more than will; for still we prove	120	
	Much in our vows, but little in our love.		
DUKE	But died thy sister of her love, my boy?		
CESARIO	I am all the daughters of my father's house,		
	And all the brothers too – and yet I know not.		
	Sir, shall I to this lady?	125	
DUKE	Ay, that's the theme.		
	To her in haste. Give her this jewel; say		
	My love can give no place, bide no denay.		

[Exeunt.

Because boy-actors played female roles, Shakespeare often developed situations in which the woman disguises herself as a boy or a man, thus making the boy-actor more convincing.

The scene you have just read is an example of this, though you were not told in the introductory note. Now let us look at the situation from the point of view of the audience who know that Cesario is not a youth, but a young woman, Viola, in disguise. Not only that, but she is in love with Orsino herself, yet cannot openly declare it. She therefore expresses her love in an indirect way by saying:
My father had a daughter lov'd a man
– but, of course, the meaning is lost on Orsino who has no idea that she is a woman.

We, the audience, however, recognise Viola's double meaning and the scene becomes rich in what is called DRAMATIC IRONY – a technique often found in Shakespeare and particularly in plays involving disguise.

It is the effect created by the audience knowing 'the truth', but the characters (or some of them) remaining in ignorance of it.

Read the Cesario-Orsino scene again and follow through some of the uses of dramatic irony with the help of these questions:

1 In which line does Viola (Cesario) first speak about herself indirectly?

2 In lines 94 – 104 Orsino says that a woman's love is less constant and passionate than a man's. In which line does Viola disagree with him?

3 Can you quote the most obvious example of irony from lines 107–111?

4 If we take lines 113–118 to refer to Viola herself, what do they tell us about her character? Use as much detail of the speech as you can in your answer.

5 In lines 119–121 Viola is critical of the attitude of 'we men' towards loving. What exactly is she saying?

6 Viola has a twin brother, Sebastian, who has been shipwrecked and may – or may not – have been drowned. In which line does she refer to him?

7 Why do you think Viola ends her reference to daughters and brothers with: Sir, shall I to this lady?

8 What could be made of the fact that Sebastian is Viola's identical twin and turns up later in the play?

55

From *The Merchant of Venice*
A POUND OF FLESH

This play still arouses controversy when it is performed, as it presents Shylock, the Jewish money-lender, in a less favourable light than the Christians. In doing so it reflects the prejudices common in Elizabethan England, though, of course, we do not need to accept them ourselves. The very study of a scene in which racial and religious bias is so obviously displayed can help us to question our own attitudes.

In order to woo PORTIA, a rich Venetian heiress, BASSANIO has to borrow money from his close friend, ANTONIO.

Antonio's money, however, was tied up in ships that were still at sea and as a temporary measure he borrowed the money from a Jewish money-lender named SHYLOCK. The loan was drawn up in a bond which stated that if Antonio could not repay the money by a certain date, he must forfeit one pound of his flesh to Shylock.

Antonio's ships are wrecked; he cannot repay the loan and in a court of law Shylock demands his pound of flesh.

Portia however, has decided to intervene. Disguised as a learned lawyer from Rome (and accompanied by her maid NERISSA – disguised as a clerk) she undertakes the defence of Antonio.

The Duke reads the letter from the old lawyer Bellario, explaining that he has asked a brilliant young doctor named Balthazar (Portia) to deputize for him.

Characters

DUKE OF VENICE

PORTIA	Bassanio's wife
SHYLOCK	a Jewish money-lender
ANTONIO	friend to Bassanio
BASSANIO	a Venetian
NERISSA	Portia's waiting-maid
GRATIANO	Nerissa's husband
A CLERK	

ACT 4, SCENE 1

DUKE   Meantime, the court shall hear Bellario's letter.

CLERK   *[Reads.]* "Your Grace shall understand that at the
receipt of your letter I am very sick; but in the instant
that your messenger came, in loving visitation was   150
with me a young doctor of Rome – his name is
Balthazar. I acquainted him with the cause in
controversy between the Jew and Antonio the
merchant; we turn'd o'er many books together; he is
furnished with my opinion which, better'd with his   155
own learning – the greatness whereof I cannot enough
commend – comes with him at my importunity to fill
up your Grace's request in my stead. I beseech you let
his lack of years be no impediment to let him lack a
reverend estimation, for I never knew so young a body   160
with so old a head. I leave him to your gracious
acceptance, whose trial shall better publish his commendation."

Enter PORTIA *for* BALTHAZAR, *dressed like
a Doctor of Laws.*

DUKE   You hear the learn'd Bellario, what he writes;
And here, I take it, is the doctor come.   165
Give me your hand; come you from old Bellario?

PORTIA   I did, my lord.

157 importunity:
earnest request
160 reverend
estimation: to be
thought of with
respect
162 commendation:
worth

DUKE	You are welcome; take your place.
	Are you acquainted with the difference
	That holds this present question in the court? 170
PORTIA	I am informed thoroughly of the cause.
	Which is the merchant here, and which the Jew?
DUKE	Antonio and old Shylock, both stand forth.
PORTIA	Is your name Shylock?
SHYLOCK	Shylock is my name. 175
PORTIA	Of a strange nature is the suit you follow;
	Yet in such rule that the Venetian law
	Cannot impugn you as you do proceed.
	You stand within his danger, do you not?
ANTONIO	Ay, so he says. 180
PORTIA	Do you confess the bond?
ANTONIO	I do.
PORTIA	Then must the Jew be merciful.
SHYLOCK	On what compulsion must I? Tell me that.

178 *impugn*: blame, accuse

PORTIA	The quality of mercy is not strain'd;	185
	It droppeth as the gentle rain from heaven	
	Upon the place beneath. It is twice blest:	
	It blesseth him that gives and him that takes.	
	'Tis mightiest in the mightiest; it becomes	
	The throned monarch better than his crown;	190
	His sceptre shows the force of temporal power,	
	The attribute to awe and majesty,	
	Wherein doth sit the dread and fear of kings;	
	But mercy is above this sceptred sway,	
	It is enthroned in the hearts of kings,	195
	It is an attribute to God himself;	
	And earthly power doth then show likest God's	
	When mercy seasons justice. Therefore, Jew,	
	Though justice be thy plea, consider this—	
	That in the course of justice none of us	200
	Should see salvation; we do pray for mercy,	
	And that same prayer doth teach us all to render	
	The deeds of mercy. I have spoke thus much	
	To mitigate the justice of thy plea,	
	Which if thou follow, this strict court of Venice	205
	Must needs give sentence 'gainst the merchant there.	
SHYLOCK	My deeds upon my head! I crave the law,	
	The penalty and forfeit of my bond.	
PORTIA	Is he not able to discharge the money?	
BASSANIO	Yes; here I tender it for him in the court;	210
	Yea, twice the sum; if that will not suffice,	
	I will be bound to pay it ten times o'er	
	On forfeit of my hands, my head, my heart;	
	If this will not suffice, it must appear	
	That malice bears down truth. And, I beseech you,	215
	Wrest once the law to your authority;	
	To do a great right do a little wrong,	
	And curb this cruel devil of his will.	
PORTIA	It must not be; there is no power in Venice	
	Can alter a decree established;	220
	'Twill be recorded for a precedent,	
	And many an error, by the same example,	
	Will rush into the state; it cannot be.	
SHYLOCK	A Daniel come to judgment! Yea, a Daniel!	
	O wise young judge, how I do honour thee!	225
PORTIA	I pray you, let me look upon the bond.	
SHYLOCK	Here 'tis, most reverend Doctor; here it is.	
PORTIA	Shylock, there's thrice thy money off'red thee.	
SHYLOCK	An oath, an oath! I have an oath in heaven.	
	Shall I lay perjury upon my soul?	230
	No, not for Venice.	
PORTIA	Why, this bond is forfeit;	
	And lawfully by this the Jew may claim	
	A pound of flesh, to be by him cut off	
	Nearest the merchant's heart. Be merciful.	235
	Take thrice thy money; bid me tear the bond.	
SHYLOCK	When it is paid according to the tenour.	
	It doth appear you are a worthy judge;	
	You know the law; your exposition	
	Hath been most sound; I charge you by the law,	240
	Whereof you are a well-deserving pillar,	
	Proceed to judgment. By my soul I swear	
	There is no power in the tongue of man	
	To alter me. I stay here on my bond.	

185 *is not strain'd*: is not forced

189 *it becomes*: it suits, it is becoming (appropriate) to

198 *seasons*: modifies

204 *mitigate*: soften

230 *perjury*: breaking an oath

237 *tenour*: terms of the bond

239 *exposition*: speech, argument

ANTONIO	Most heartily I do beseech the court 245
	To give the judgment.
PORTIA	Why then, thus it is:
	You must prepare your bosom for his knife.
SHYLOCK	O noble judge! O excellent young man!
PORTIA	For the intent and purpose of the law 250
	Hath full relation to the penalty,
	Which here appeareth due upon the bond.
SHYLOCK	'Tis very true. O wise and upright judge,
	How much more elder art thou than thy looks!
PORTIA	Therefore, lay bare your bosom. 255
SHYLOCK	Ay, his breast —
	So says the bond; doth it not, noble judge?
	"Nearest his heart", those are the very words.
PORTIA	It is so. Are there balance here to weigh
	The flesh? 260
SHYLOCK	I have them ready.
PORTIA	Have by some surgeon, Shylock, on your charge,
	To stop his wounds, lest he do bleed to death.
SHYLOCK	Is it so nominated in the bond?
PORTIA	It is not so express'd, but what of that? 265
	'Twere good you do so much for charity.
SHYLOCK	I cannot find it; 'tis not in the bond.
PORTIA	You, merchant, have you anything to say?
ANTONIO	But little: I am arm'd and well prepar'd.
	Give me your hand Bassanio; fare you well. 270
	Grieve not that I am fall'n to this for you,
	For herein Fortune shows herself more kind
	Than is her custom. It is still her use
	To let the wretched man outlive his wealth,
	To view with hollow eye and wrinkled brow 275
	An age of poverty; from which ling'ring penance
	Of such misery doth she cut me off.
	Commend me to your honourable wife;
	Tell her the process of Antonio's end;
	Say how I lov'd you; speak me fair in death; 280
	And, when the tale is told, bid her be judge
	Whether Bassanio had not once a love.
	Repent but you that you shall lose your friend,
	And he repents not that he pays your debt;
	For if the Jew do cut but deep enough, 285
	I'll pay it instantly with all my heart.
BASSANIO	Antonio, I am married to a wife
	Which is as dear to me as life itself;
	But life itself, my wife, and all the world,
	Are not with me esteem'd above thy life; 290
	I would lose all, ay, sacrifice them all
	Here to this devil, to deliver you.
PORTIA	Your wife would give you little thanks for that,
	If she were by to hear you make the offer.
GRATIANO	I have a wife who I protest I love; 295
	I would she were in heaven, so she could
	Entreat some power to change this currish Jew.
NERISSA	'Tis well you offer it behind her back;
	The wish would make else an unquiet house.
SHYLOCK	[Aside.] These be the Christian husbands! I have a 300
	daughter —
	Would any of the stock of Barrabas
	Had been her husband, rather than a Christian! —
	We trifle time; I pray thee pursue sentence.

273 *use*: custom

276 *penance*:——
punishment for
sin

PORTIA	A pound of that same merchant's flesh is thine.	305
	The court awards it and the law doth give it.	
SHYLOCK	Most rightful judge!	
PORTIA	And you must cut this flesh from off his breast.	
	The law allows it and the court awards it.	
SHYLOCK	Most learned judge! A sentence! Come, prepare.	310
PORTIA	Tarry a little; there is something else.	
	This bond doth give thee here no jot of blood:	
	The words expressly are "a pound of flesh".	
	Take then thy bond, take thou thy pound of flesh;	
	But, in the cutting it, if thou dost shed	315
	One drop of Christian blood, thy lands and goods	
	Are, by the laws of Venice, confiscate	
	Unto the state of Venice.	
GRATIANO	O upright judge! Mark, Jew. O learned judge!	
SHYLOCK	Is that the law?	320
PORTIA	Thyself shalt see the act;	
	For, as thou urgest justice, be assur'd	
	Thou shalt have justice, more than thou desir'st.	
GRATIANO	O learned judge! Mark, Jew. A learned judge.	
SHYLOCK	I take this offer then: pay the bond thrice,	325
	And let the Christian go.	
BASSIANO	Here is the money.	
PORTIA	Soft!	
	The Jew shall have all justice. Soft! No haste.	
	He shall have nothing but the penalty.	330
GRATIANO	O Jew! an upright judge, a learned judge!	
PORTIA	Therefore, prepare thee to cut off the flesh.	
	Shed thou no blood, nor cut thou less nor more	
	But just a pound of flesh; if thou tak'st more	
	Or less than a just pound – be it but so much	335
	As makes it light or heavy in the substance,	
	Or the division of the twentieth part	
	Of one poor scruple; nay, if the scale do turn	
	But in the estimation of a hair –	
	Thou diest, and all thy goods are confiscate.	340
GRATIANO	A second Daniel, a Daniel, Jew!	
	Now, infidel, I have you on the hip.	
PORTIA	Why doth the Jew pause? Take thy forfeiture.	
SHYLOCK	Give me my principal, and let me go.	
BASSIANO	I have it ready for thee; here it is.	345
PORTIA	He hath refus'd it in the open court;	
	He shall have merely justice, and his bond.	
GRATIANO	A Daniel still say I, a second Daniel!	
	I thank thee, Jew, for teaching me that word.	
SHYLOCK	Shall I not have barely my principal?	350
PORTIA	Thou shalt have nothing but the forfeiture	
	To be so taken at thy peril, Jew.	
SHYLOCK	Why, then the devil give him good of it!	
	I'll stay no longer question.	
PORTIA	Tarry, Jew.	355
	The law hath yet another hold on you.	
	It is enacted in the laws of Venice,	
	If it be proved against an alien	
	That by direct or indirect attempts	
	He seek the life of any citizen,	360
	The party 'gainst the which he doth contrive	
	Shall seize one half his goods; the other half	
	Comes to the privy coffer of the state;	

338 *scruple*: 20 grains in weight

342 *on the hip*: at a disadvantage (derived from a wrestling term)

344 *principal*: sum of money owed

	And the offender's life lies in the mercy	
	Of the Duke only, 'gainst all other voice.	365
	In which predicament, I say, thou stand'st;	
	For it appears by manifest proceeding	
	That indirectly, and directly too,	
	Thou hast contrived against the very life	
	Of the defendant; and thou hast incurr'd	370
	The danger formerly by me rehears'd.	
	Down, therefore, and beg mercy of the Duke.	
GRATIANO	Beg that thou mayst have leave to hang thyself;	
	And yet, thy wealth being forfeit to the state,	
	Thou has not left the value of a cord;	375
	Therefore thou must be hang'd at the state's charge.	
DUKE	That thou shalt see the difference of our spirit,	
	I pardon thee thy life before thou ask it.	
	For half thy wealth, it is Antonio's;	
	The other half comes to the general state,	380
	Which humbleness may drive unto a fine.	
PORTIA	Ay, for the state; not for Antonio.	
SHYLOCK	Nay, take my life and all, pardon not that.	
	You take my house when you do take the prop	
	That doth sustain my house; you take my life	385
	When you do take the means whereby I live.	
PORTIA	What mercy can you render him, Antonio?	
GRATIANO	A halter gratis; nothing else, for God's sake!	
ANTONIO	So please my lord the Duke and all the court	
	To quit the fine for one half of his goods;	390
	I am content, so he will let me have	
	The other half in use, to render it	
	Upon his death unto the gentleman	
	That lately stole his daughter –	
	Two things provided more: that, for this favour,	395
	He presently become a Christian;	
	The other, that he do record a gift,	
	Here in the court, of all he dies possess'd	
	Unto his son Lorenzo and his daughter.	
DUKE	He shall do this, or else I do recant	400
	The pardon that I late pronounced here.	
PORTIA	Art thou contented, Jew? What dost thou say?	
SHYLOCK	I am content.	
PORTIA	Clerk, draw a deed of gift.	
SHYLOCK	I pray you, give me leave to go from hence;	405
	I am not well; send the deed after me	
	And I will sign it.	
DUKE	Get thee gone, but do it.	
GRATIANO	In christ'ning shalt thou have two god-fathers;	
	Had I been judge, thou shouldst have had ten more,	410
	To bring thee to the gallows, not to the font.	
	[Exit Shylock.	

388 *halter gratis*: a noose, free of charge

392 *in use*: in trust

397 *he do record a gift*: formally agrees to make a gift

400 *recant*: take back

- What do you think of Portia's argument – that Shylock must not shed any blood?
- Is Shylock fairly treated?
- Where did your sympathies lie during the scene?
- How does disguise produce dramatic irony?

- What exactly is Portia saying about mercy in her famous speech (lines 185–203)? Can you express the meaning in your own words?
- What part does Gratiano play in the scene?

An Interview with
DR JOHN HALL

PRESENTER

We'll now return to Stratford upon Avon and retrace our steps a little. Shakespeare, you will remember, had three children: Susanna and the twins, Judith and Hamnet. When Susanna was twenty-four she married a young Cambridge graduate, Dr John Hall, who practised medicine in Stratford. As Dr Hall must have had an intimate knowledge of Shakespeare's later life in Stratford, he will be the subject of our last interview.

INTERVIEWER

Dr Hall, we've learnt a lot about Shakespeare as a boy and about the theatre he worked in, but we haven't yet discussed his life in Stratford after he achieved fame in London. Do you think you can fill in some of the gaps in our knowledge?

DR HALL

I'll do my best! I didn't arrive in Stratford till 1600 and by then everyone knew who William Shakespeare was. He was the prosperous poet and playwright who had actually met Queen Elizabeth!

INTERVIEWER

Did he show any signs of being successful and well-off?

DR HALL

Oh yes. He owned arable and pasture lands just outside Stratford, and he had inherited the house in Henley Street where he was born; but what set him above everyone else was his buying the Great House of New Place – the largest house in Stratford. It's true that he bought it for £60, but it was in a pretty dilapidated state and needed a lot of money spending on it to restore it to its former glory.

INTERVIEWER

A document was discovered recently to show that Shakespeare actually sold the stone that was left over from the rebuilding back to the Stratford council – so he was thrifty as well as rich!

DR HALL

Ha! I can well believe it! He was no fool where money was concerned!

INTERVIEWER

Thrifty he may have been, but he has also been described – and I quote – as 'gentle', 'friendly', 'civil', 'dear-lov'd'. The son of one of his fellow actors also described him as 'a handsome, well-shaped man, very good company and of a very ready and pleasant smooth wit'.

DR HALL

He was also a gentleman. You should add that.

INTERVIEWER

Aren't we all gentlemen?

DR HALL

We don't all have a coat of arms. It is that that entitles a man to the status of 'gentleman'.

INTERVIEWER

Things have obviously changed since your day, Dr Hall. But what was the significance of a coat of arms and how did Shakespeare acquire one?

DR HALL

A coat of arms set a man above his fellows: it was a sign of rank and of achievement. It became his family's crest and could be displayed at the entrance of his house. How did William acquire one? Well,

62

strictly speaking, it was old John who was awarded the honour for his services as bailiff to Stratford, but perhaps Will's success as a playwright had something to do with it as well; and when John died in 1601 the title became William's own.

INTERVIEWER
But not, unfortunately, to be passed on to William's own son – for we know that Hamnet died in 1596, only two months before the coat of arms was awarded.

DR HALL
It cast a shadow over his life – over all their lives. What is a coat of arms and the status of gentleman beside the loss of one's only son?

INTERVIEWER
But what is interesting is that the years we are discussing – 1596–97 – when he acquired the coat of arms, bought New Place and when Hamnet died, were the years before his greatest period as a dramatist. The tragedies were still to come and he had about fifteen years of theatrical life ahead of him. Did he visit his family in Stratford during these years?

DR HALL
Yes, of course. You see, he lived in two worlds – the world of London: theatres, the court and his patron; and the world of Stratford: family, friends and lawsuits he undertook about his property and his land.

INTERVIEWER
The professional and the private. Did he keep the two worlds strictly apart?

DR HALL
No, he occasionally attended lawsuits in London and he often had his London friends come to stay with him in Stratford. He lived easily in both worlds and loved both. His will testifies to that.

INTERVIEWER
You mean that he remembered friends in the theatre and the literary world as well as his friends and family in Stratford?

DR HALL
Yes. Take memorial rings, for example –

INTERVIEWER
What were memorial rings? We don't have the term in the twentieth century.

DR HALL
Memorial rings? These were rings worn in memory of a friend who had died. It was customary for a man to leave money in his will for his friends to buy memorial rings with. Well, Will left money for memorial rings both to his close friends in Stratford, like Hamnet Sadler whom Will had known since they were boys together, and to his old acquaintances of the Lord Chamberlain's Men, like Richard Burbage and several others. And he left £10 to the poor of Stratford.

INTERVIEWER
What often puzzles people of my day is why he left his second-best bed to his wife, Anne. Why didn't he leave her his best bed?

DR HALL
The best bed was always kept for visitors! The second-best bed was the bed William and Anne had shared during their married life. Naturally, that should go to Anne.

INTERVIEWER
It was also, presumably, the bed in which he died. It was a strange coincidence that he should die on April 23rd, the day of his birth fifty-two years earlier.

DR HALL
Saint George's Day.

INTERVIEWER
Was it an impressive funeral?

DR HALL
As you might expect for a man who had achieved so much and had retained so many friends. He was buried in our parish church, Holy Trinity, not a mile from where he was born. The church in which he had been baptised. Anne commissioned the sculpture of William which was placed in the niche above his grave. Is it there still?

INTERVIEWER
It is. Very little has changed. The bust in the niche. The tomb covered by the inscribed stone:
>Good friend for Jesus sake forbear
>To dig the dust enclosed here;
>Blest be the man that spares these stones,
>And cursed be he that moves my bones

DR HALL
Not Will's finest lines, but necessary ones. There was a shortage of burial space in the churchyard and the sexton used to dig up old graves and throw the

bones in the charnel house nearby. Has Will been spared that?

INTERVIEWER
He has. So far as we know, his bones lie there still.

DR HALL
And what of Will's reputation since his bones were laid to rest? Has it survived into your century?

INTERVIEWER
It has survived and grown. If you were to stay in London for a month, you could probably see seven or eight of his plays performed.

DR HALL
How I wish I could! But it's difficult for us Elizabethans to keep up appearances in the twentieth century. Time is running out and I think I'd better be going. Any last question you would like to ask me before I take my leave?

"a handsome well-shaped man"

INTERVIEWER
Yes, there is one question that we have always had a burning desire to have answered. What did Shakespeare die of?

DR HALL
It's all in my medical records. Why not consult them?

INTERVIEWER
They haven't survived. Can't you tell us?

DR HALL
Would it add to your understanding of the plays if I did?

INTERVIEWER
I suppose not.

DR HALL
Then let it remain a closed book. In Prospero's words:
>We are such stuff
>As dreams are made on, and our little life
>Is rounded with a sleep.
I leave you to your dreams and go back to my sleep.

INTERVIEWER
Thank you, Dr Hall. Sleep well!

PRESENTER

Shakespeare died in 1616. By 1623 two of his ex-colleagues from the Lord Chamberlain's Men had collected all his plays and published them in one volume, called the First Folio. Scholars began to study and compare the various texts. Biographers got to work, piecing together the life of Shakespeare from scanty records and doubtful anecdotes. Critics began to advance their 'interpretations' of the plays. Stratford became a town of international pilgrimage where annually thousands of visitors tramped through the Birthplace in Henley Street, gazed at the site where New Place had once stood and walked up to the chancel rail in Trinity Church to read the inscription on the tomb. Meanwhile, in all parts of the world, the plays were being performed, not always strictly as Shakespeare had originally intended them. There have been modern dress versions, rock musical versions, operatic versions, film and television versions, versions on ice – as well as versions in every major foreign language in the world. Century by century, year by year, the movement seems to gain momentum. What is the appeal that Shakespeare makes to each new generation? Is it a genuine appeal, or is it artificially fostered by examination boards? Starting Shakespeare is just the beginning of your answer.

CHECKPOINT

Questions for written or oral answers on the interview with Dr John Hall.

1 Where had John Hall studied medicine?

2 By 1600 what property did Shakespeare own in Stratford?

3 Quote four words or phrases used to describe Shakespeare by people who knew him personally.

4 To whom was the coat of arms originally awarded?

5 Which family deaths occurred in 1596 and 1601?

6 What was a 'memorial ring'?

7 Name two friends of Shakespeare who received memorial rings in his will.

8 Why did Anne receive the second-best bed?

9 How old was Shakespeare when he died?

10 What coincidence was there about the date of his death?

One version of Measure for Measure

SHAKESPEARE'S FAMILY TREE

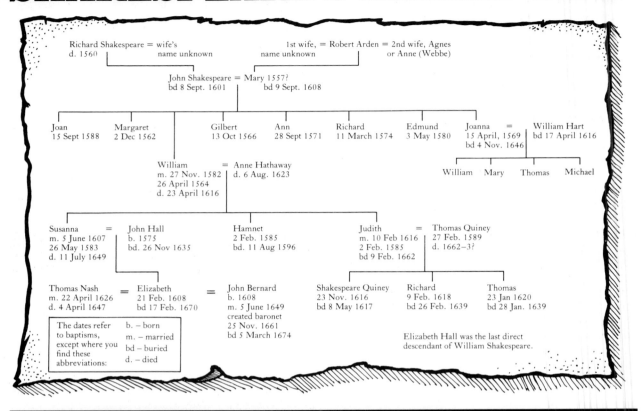

Richard Shakespeare = wife's name unknown
d. 1560

1st wife, = Robert Arden = 2nd wife, Agnes name unknown or Anne (Webbe)

John Shakespeare = Mary 1557?
bd 8 Sept. 1601   bd 9 Sept. 1608

Joan 15 Sept 1588
Margaret 2 Dec 1562
Gilbert 13 Oct 1566
Ann 28 Sept 1571
Richard 11 March 1574
Edmund 3 May 1580
Joanna = William Hart
15 April, 1569   bd 17 April 1616
bd 4 Nov. 1646

William   Mary   Thomas   Michael

William = Anne Hathaway
m. 27 Nov. 1582   d. 6 Aug. 1623
26 April 1564
d. 23 April 1616

Susanna = John Hall
m. 5 June 1607   b. 1575
26 May 1583   bd. 26 Nov 1635
d. 11 July 1649

Hamnet 2 Feb. 1585
bd. 11 Aug 1596

Judith = Thomas Quiney
m. 10 Feb 1616   27 Feb. 1589
2 Feb. 1585   d. 1662–3?
bd 9 Feb. 1662

Thomas Nash = Elizabeth = John Bernard
m. 22 April 1626   21 Feb. 1608   b. 1608
d. 4 April 1647   bd 17 Feb. 1670   m. 5 June 1649
created baronet
25 Nov. 1661
bd 5 March 1674

Shakespeare Quiney 23 Nov. 1616   bd 8 May 1617
Richard 9 Feb. 1618   bd 26 Feb. 1639
Thomas 23 Jan 1620   bd 28 Jan. 1639

The dates refer to baptisms, except where you find these abbreviations:
b. – born
m. – married
bd – buried
d. – died

Elizabeth Hall was the last direct descendant of William Shakespeare.

A Shakespeare Chronology

1558	Accession of Queen Elizabeth I
1564	William Shakespeare born, 23 April
1576	The Theatre, London's first playhouse, opened
1582	Shakespeare married Anne Hathaway, 27 November
1583	Shakespeare's daughter, Susanna, baptised 26 May
1585	Shakespeare's twins, Hamnet and Judith, baptised 2 February
1585–92	The Lost Years
1590–91	Shakespeare's first plays performed (*Henry VI, Parts 2 and 3*)
1592–94	Plague in London. Playhouses closed
1593	'Venus and Adonis' (poem) published
1594	'The Rape of Lucrece' (poem) published
1594	Shakespeare's first plays printed
1596	Hamnet died
1596	Shakespeare family granted a coat of arms
1597	Shakespeare bought New Place
1599	The Globe Theatre opened
1601	John Shakespeare died
1603	Death of Queen Elizabeth. Accession of James I
1603	Plague. Playhouses closed
1609	Shakespeare's sonnets published
1613	Globe Theatre destroyed by fire
1614	Second Globe opened
1616	Shakespeare died, 23 April
1623	Anne Shakespeare died
1623	The collected plays printed in the First Folio
1879	Shakespeare Memorial Theatre opened in Stratford upon Avon

Notes on the Family Tree:

- There is no record of John Shakespeare's marriage because registers in the village church where he was married do not commence till later.

- Similarly, there is no record of Anne Hathaway's christening because she seems to have been born before 1558 when baptismal registers commence.

- It is generally agreed that William Shakespeare was born on 23 April, 1564, because his baptism is registered on 26 April – the customary three days after the birth.

Some questions

1 How many brothers and sisters had William?

2 By how many years and months did Anne Shakespeare survive her husband?

3 Exactly how old was Shakespeare when the twins were born?

4 How old was Hamnet when he died?

5 To what grand old age did Judith, Shakespeare's daughter, live?

6 What family events are recorded for 1616?

7 In a few sentences, outline the life of Elizabeth Hall.

8 What would Elizabeth's title be when her husband was created a baronet?

9 How many grandchildren did Shakespeare have?

10 What family tragedies had Judith to bear?

What else can you learn from a study of the dates on the family tree?

WHO'S WHO

Part of the appeal that Shakespeare makes to each generation of playgoers is his gift for creating characters – of every type and from all walks of life. He wrote at least thirty-six plays and according to a recent count, created over 800 characters.

Throughout the plays we come across speeches in which the characters either describe themselves or are described by others in order that we, the audience, might get to know and understand them more completely.

Twelve quotations from these speeches follow, each portraying some aspect of a prominent character. Before the quotations, the twelve characters are briefly summed up – but not in the same order as the quotations.

Can you find the quotation that fits each character? Be careful, there are one or two misleading 'clues'!

PUCK   A mischievous sprite or goblin in *A Midsummer Night's Dream* who plays tricks on simple, trusting people.

KATHERINA   In *The Taming of the Shrew* Katherina is young, beautiful, and from a good family. She would make a wonderful wife, except that she is outspoken to the point of rudeness.

FALSTAFF   A rogue of an old man with a great sense of humour and over-fond of eating and drinking. He is disapproved of by King Henry IV because he is said to be leading young Prince Hal astray.

RICHARD III   Richard, Duke of Gloucester, is a hunchback and extremely conscious of his lack of attraction for women.

ROSALIND   Living rough in the Forest of Arden, she thinks it wiser to disguise herself as a man. She's in *As You Like It*.

HORATIO   This is the Horatio who is called to witness the Ghost in *Hamlet*. Hamlet values him as a friend because he has an even temper and takes the ups and downs of life in his stride.

CLEOPATRA   Queen of Egypt and in love with Mark Antony. She is so fascinating that almost everything she does seems attractive.

YORICK   He appears in *Hamlet* as a skull! He was the jester at the Danish court and his bones are unearthed when the grave-digger is preparing a new grave.

CORIOLANUS   Before his attack on Rome he is described as a man of ruthless power and overwhelming pride.

DESDEMONA   According to her father, she is a shy, retiring girl. Brought up in the cultured society of Venice, how could she fall in love with Othello, a man of a different race whom she is actually afraid of?

MERCUTIO   In this speech Mercutio claims to be describing the quarrelsome temperament of his friend Benvolio, but he is actually depicting himself.

CORDELIA   Cordelia, the sensitive and loving daughter of King Lear, has received a letter that caused her some pain. The Gentleman who delivered the letter describes how Cordelia struggled to hide her tears.

1 But I – that am not shap'd for sportive tricks,
Nor made to court an amorous looking-glass –
I – that am rudely stamp'd, and want love's majesty
To strut before a wanton ambling nymph –
I – that am curtail'd of this fair proportion,
Cheated of feature by dissembling nature,
Deform'd, unfinishe'd, sent before my time
Into this breathing world scarce half made up,
And that so lamely and unfashionable
That dogs bark at me as I halt by them –

2 And sometime lurk I in a gossip's bowl
In very likeness of a roasted crab,
And, when she drinks, against her lips I bob,
And on her withered dewlap pour the ale.
The wisest aunt, telling the saddest tale,
Sometime for three-foot stool mistaketh me;
Then slip I from her bum, down topples she,
And 'tailor' cries, and falls into a cough;
And then the whole quire hold their hips and laugh,
And waxen in their mirth, and neeze, and swear
A merrier hour was never wasted there.

3 A man that Fortune's buffets and rewards
Hast ta'en with equal thanks; and blest are those
Whose blood and judgment are so well comeddled
That they are not a pipe for Fortune's finger
To sound what stop she please. Give me that man
That is not passion's slave, and I will wear him
In my heart's core, ay, in my heart of heart,
As I do thee.

4   Were it not better,
Because that I am more than common tall,
That I did suit me all points like a man?
A gallant curtle-axe upon my thigh,
A boar spear in my hand; and – in my heart
Lie there what hidden woman's fear there will –

5 With wealth enough, and young and beauteous;
Brought up as best becomes a gentlewoman;
Her only fault, and that is faults enough,
Is – that she is intolerable curst,
And shrewd and froward so beyond all measure
That, were my state far worser than it is,
I would not wed her for a mine of gold.

6   I saw her once
Hop forty paces through the public street;
And, having lost her breath, she spoke, and panted,
That she did make defect perfection,
And, breathless, pow'r breathe forth . . .
Age cannot wither her, nor custom stale
Her infinite variety. Other women cloy
The appetites they feed, but she makes hungry
Where most she satisfies;

7 Thou art violently carried away from grace; there is a devil haunts thee in the likeness of an old fat man; a tun of man is thy companion. Why dost thou converse with that trunk of humours, that bolting-hutch of beastliness, that swoll'n parcel of dropsies, that huge bombard of sack, that stuff'd cloak-bag of guts, that roasted Manningtree ox with the pudding in his belly, that reverend vice, that grey iniquity, that father ruffian, that vanity in years? Wherein is he good, but to taste sack and drink it? wherein neat and cleanly, but to carve a capon and eat it? wherein cunning, but in craft? wherein crafty, but in villainy? wherein villainous, but in all things? wherein worthy, but in nothing?

8 Thou! why, thou wilt quarrel with a man that hath a hair more or a hair less in his beard than thou hast. Thou wilt quarrel with a man for cracking nuts, having no other reason but because thou hast hazel eyes. What eye but such an eye would spy out such a quarrel? Thy head is as full of quarrels as an egg is full of meat; and yet thy head hath been beaten as addle as an egg for quarrelling. Thou hast quarrell'd with a man for coughing in the street, because he hath wakened thy dog that hath lain asleep in the sun.

9 The tartness of his face sours ripe grapes; when he walks, he moves like an engine and the ground shrinks before his treading. He is able to pierce a corslet with his eye, talks like a knell, and his hum is a battery. He sits in his state as a thing made for Alexander. What he bids be done is finish'd with his bidding. He wants nothing of a god but eternity, and a heaven to throne in.

10   You have seen
Sunshine and rain at once; her smiles and tears
Were like a better way. Those happy smilets
That play'd on her ripe lip seem'd not to know
What guests were in her eyes, which parted thence
As pearls from diamonds dropp'd.

11 I knew him, Horatio: a fellow of infinite jest, of most excellent fancy; he hath borne me on his back a thousand times. And now how abhorred in my imagination it is! My gorge rises at it. Here hung those lips that I have kiss'd I know not how oft. Where be your gibes now, your gambols, your songs, your flashes of merriment that were wont to set the table on a roar? Not one now to mock your own grinning – quite chap-fall'n?

12   A maiden never bold,
Of spirit so still and quiet that her motion
Blush'd at herself; and she – in spite of nature,
Of years, of country, credit, every thing –
To fall in love with what she fear'd to look on!

FINDING OUT MORE

- Here's an opportunity for doing some research yourself.

- Below is a list of what might be called *mini-topics* – that is, they are meant to be treated briefly, not at full length.

- They are intended to fill in some of the gaps in our knowledge of Shakespeare and the Elizabethan theatre.

- Several books are suggested, but if these are not available, look for other books on Shakespeare and see if these cover the topics you have chosen. *You will find encyclopedias particularly useful.*

- Change your topic to fit in with the information your book gives.

- Use the index of a book to find the pages you need.

- Work singly, in pairs or in groups. Present your work in a written or an oral form.

- If you can illustrate your work with photographs, models or photocopies, so much the better.

- Use the resources of your school library and the local public library. Don't be afraid of asking a librarian to help you find the book you want. If it has to be ordered from another library, you can put in a special request slip for it.

SOME USEFUL BOOKS FOR THE TOPICS:

William Shakespeare: A Compact Documentary Life
    S Schoenbaum   Oxford University Press
Shakespeare's Life and Times
    Roland Mushat Frye   Faber
Shakespeare
    Anthony Burgess   Penguin
Understanding Shakespeare
    G B Harrison   Penguin
The Shakespeares
    Nathaniel Harris   J M Dent & Sons
Shakespeare
    Kenneth Grose and B T Oxley
A New Companion to Shakespeare Studies
    Kenneth Muir and Samuel Schoenbaum
    Cambridge University Press
The Story of the Elizabethan Boy-Actors
    Katherine Hudson   Oxford University Press
Shakespeare's Second Globe
    C Walter Hodges
Shakespeare: An Illustrated Dictionary
    Stanley Wells Oxford University Press

Your project work can be divided into a number of stages:

1   Having chosen your topic, find the book or books you need.

2   In these books, look for the pages that give you the information you want. Make good use of the index. It can save a lot of time.

3   Don't copy large sections of the book – make notes and include quotations if you wish.

4   Write up your material in your own words.

THE MINI TOPICS

1 The Boys' Companies were, for a time, great rivals of the adult acting companies. Find out about THE CHILDREN OF THE CHAPEL ROYAL and THE CHILDREN OF PAUL'S.

The Story of the Elizabethan Boy-Actors (pages 13–33)

2 Find out what you can about the kidnapping of boys to sing and act in the Children's Companies. You could include the story of the kidnapping of Master Thomas Clifton in 1600.

The Story of the Elizabethan Boy-Actors (pages 48–57)

3 Find out what you can about Elizabethan BEAR-BAITING and similar entertainments, which were popular on the South Bank.

 Shakespeare's Life and Times (No. 17)

4 Find out what you can about the great comic actors in Shakespeare's day: RICHARD TARLETON (*Life & Times*, No. 20); WILLIAM KEMPE (*Documentary Life*, 210–11; *Life & Times*, No. 61); ROBERT ARMIN (*Life & Times*, No. 62). Look them up in the index of *Shakespeare* by Burgess.

5 You learnt something about Shakespeare's schooldays in the interview with John Shakespeare. Find out more about the life of a typical Elizabethan boy.

 Shakespeare Burgess (pages 27–44)
The Shakespeares (pages 40–48)

6 Some of Shakespeare's plays were first published in separate editions, called QUARTOS. Later, the plays were collected and published in a single volume, called the FIRST FOLIO. Other Folio editions followed. Find out what you can about the Quarto and Folio editions of Shakespeare's plays.

 Shakespeare Grose and Oxley
Shakespeare's Life and Times

7 What can you discover about the theatrical companies of Shakespeare's day? You have read about THE LORD CHAMBERLAIN'S MEN and THE KING'S MEN. There were several others.

 Shakespeare (pages 30–35)

8 There are still some mysteries and problems surrounding SHAKESPEARE'S MARRIAGE. Can you find out more about the people involved, the money that was paid and the church regulations that there were in force at the time? Who was 'the other Anne'?

A Compact Documentary Life (pages 75–88)
Shakespeare Burgess (pages 56–60)

9 BEN JONSON was a fellow-dramatist and friend of Shakespeare's. He wrote an introduction to the first collected edition of Shakespeare's plays. Find out what you can about Ben Jonson's life and writings, as well as his connection with Shakespeare.

Shakespeare Burgess (pages 165–6)
Shakespeare's Life and Times (section 45)

10 Are the portraits and busts of Shakespeare true likenesses of him? Find out what you can about them and, if possible, take some photocopies to illustrate your findings.

Shakespeare's Life and Times (sections 1,2,3 & 4)

11 Elizabethan theatres like the GLOBE and the CURTAIN were the first permanent playhouses in England. How were plays presented before these theatres were built? Find out what you can about the temporary BOOTH-STAGES and the INN YARDS where plays were performed.

A New Companion to Shakespeare Studies (pages 15–19)

12 There was great rivalry between the public theatres like the Globe and the private theatres like the BLACKFRIARS and the PHOENIX. Find out what you can about the Elizabethan PRIVATE THEATRES.

A New Companion to Shakespeare Studies (pages 20–22)
Shakespeare's Life and Times (Nos. 95 & 96)

The interior of Stratford Grammar School – almost as it was in Shakespeare's day

13 Not all the details of Shakespeare's will were given in the interview with Dr John Hall. Who, for instance, got Shakespeare's sword? Find out more about the will.

A Documentary Life (pages 297–305)

14 Find out what the following people did in the Elizabethan theatre: the BOOK-KEEPER, the TIRE-MAN, the GATHERERS. Who was the MASTER OF REVELS? What was the PROMPT-BOOK and what were an author's FOUL-PAPERS?

Shakespeare Grose and Oxley (page 32)

15 What happened to SHAKESPEARE'S MANUSCRIPTS? No complete manuscript of a play by Shakespeare has survived. Find out what might have happened to them.

A Compact Documentary Life (pages 305–6)

16 Find out more about RICHARD BURBAGE, the great tragic actor in The Lord Chamberlain's Men.

Shakespeare's Life and Times (No. 60)

17 Find out what you can about Shakespeare's first patron, Henry Wriothesley, third Earl of Southampton.

A Compact Documentary Life (pages 170–73)
Shakespeare's Life and Times (No. 32)

18 Find out what you can about William's youngest brother, EDMUND, sixteen years his junior, who also became an actor.

Life and Times (No. 94); *Documentary Life* (pages 28–9)

19 The Memorial Theatre, Stratford upon Avon, is the base of the ROYAL SHAKESPEARE COMPANY. Find out what you can about the theatre's history and the plays that are being performed there.

20 If you visited Stratford upon Avon today, what would you be able to see or visit that was connected with Shakespeare?

21 Look up some of the traditional stories or anecdotes that are told about Shakespeare and re-tell them in your own words.

The Oxford Book of Literary Anecdotes
A Documentary Life (pages 96, 97, 144, 205–6)

22 Many of Shakespeare's plays end with dramatic deaths. How did the Elizabethans solve the problem of getting the bodies off the stage?

Introducing Shakespeare (pages 137–9)

23 What properties were used in the Elizabethan theatre?

Introducing Shakespeare (pages 140–44)

24 What costumes were used? Where did the theatres often get the costumes from?

Introducing Shakespeare (pages 144–5)

25 How often were plays performed? What was the repertoire of a typical Elizabethan company?

Introducing Shakespeare (pages 146–7)

26 HENSLOWE'S DIARY gives us some valuable information on Elizabethan theatres and companies. Find out more about it.

Introducing Shakespeare (pages 77–8)

27 To what extent did Elizabethan dramatists collaborate in the writing of plays? Do any of Shakespeare's plays contain scenes that might have been written by other dramatists?

Introducing Shakespeare (pages 195–6)

28 We have one scene of a play written in Shakespeare's own handwriting. Find out which play this is and where the manuscript lies at present.

Introducing Shakespeare (pages 198–9)

29 Dr John Hall was an interesting character in his own right.
Find out what you can about him.

A Documentary Life
Introducing Shakespeare (pages 137–9)

30 Find out more about great Shakespearean actors of our own day:
Lawrence Olivier, John Gielgud, Donald Wolfit, Ian McKellen, Ralph Richardson, Peggy Ashcroft, Alan Howard, Judi Dench.

31 Who was Dr Thomas Bowdler and what did he do to Shakespeare's plays?

Shakespeare: An Illustrated Dictionary.

32 Make a selection of quotations from Shakespeare from a Dictionary of Quotations.

33 Find out what you can about Shakespeare's SONNETS. What questions and problems arise from them?

34 What can you find out about films that have been made of Shakespeare's plays?

35 Set up a survey to find out which plays a certain number of people (in class, in school or outside) have read and seen. Which are the most popular of Shakespeare's plays?

The work in this section studies character, language and dramatic situation as a preparation for reading and studying a full-length play.

TRAGEDY · COMEDY · HISTORY · ROMANCE

Polonius, a character in *Hamlet*, introduces a group of actors to the royal court at Elsinore with these lines:

> *The best actors in the world, either for tragedy, comedy, history, pastoral, pastoral-comical, historical-pastoral, tragical-historical, tragical-comical-historical-pastoral . . .*

He starts off with the separate divisions of plays and ends up with a combination of all four. (Pastoral meant a play about country life).

He's exaggerating, of course, but there is some truth in what he says. Elizabethan plays often contained a mixture of dramatic elements. In Shakespeare's tragedies, you will find comedy; in the comedies, seriousness and sadness; and in the histories, tragedy and comedy alike.

The classical Greek theatre believed in what are called 'the unities'. This meant that the action of the play should not take up more than twenty-four hours; that it should happen in one place only; and that there should be a single plot or story-line.

Shakespeare didn't abide by any of these rules. His plays span weeks, months and years. The scene moves from place to place, and the plot often consists of three or four interwoven stories. He mixes fact with fiction and humour with pathos. He brought a new freedom and invention to the theatre and by doing so was able to appeal to every type of audience, from groundlings to courtiers.

Even so, in most of the plays one mood predominates and when Shakespeare's friends published his works after his death, they divided the plays into three categories: comedies, histories and tragedies. Later, scholars added a fourth category, called 'romances', and it is at these four categories that we shall look now.

TRAGEDIES

Love, ambition, power, jealousy – these are some of the themes of Shakespearean tragedy, with death predominating in the last act. At the heart of each play there is usually a single figure who is brought to a tragic end, either by circumstances or by some weakness in his own nature.

Beginning with the crude melodrama of *Titus Andronicus*, Shakespeare moved to the height of his dramatic achievement in the four great tragedies, *Hamlet*, *King Lear*, *Othello* and *Macbeth*, each remarkable for its fine language and powerful portrayal of character. These plays, together with *Antony and Cleopatra*, *Julius Caesar* and *Romeo and Juliet*, have been popular with audiences for generations and many of them have been made into successful films.

COMEDIES

The comedies are usually built around the relations of young men and women in love: their quarrels, misfortunes and eventual union. In addition to the lovers, we meet a host of humorous characters who make an audience laugh by their foolishness or wit. The plots of these plays are usually intricate, with many twists and surprises.

Some comedies are more serious than others. *The Comedy of Errors* is light-hearted and full of slapstick humour; *The Merchant of Venice* has a central character in Shylock who is more tragic than comic; and the main theme of *Measure for Measure* is undoubtedly serious. The category 'comedies' is therefore a broad one and covers several different kinds of play. *Troilus and Cressida* has at various times been described as a comedy, a tragedy and a history!

HISTORIES

Shakespeare wrote ten plays on English history and they fall into two main groups (or 'cycles') with two that don't belong to either group:

1 *Henry VI, Parts 1, 2 and 3*
   Richard III

2 *Richard II*
   Henry IV, Parts 1 and 2
   Henry V.

The two unplaced plays are *King John* and Shakespeare's last play, *Henry VIII.*

In these history plays Shakespeare is showing the qualities that are needed in a king if he is to combat enemies abroad and rebellious nobles at home. The question is often asked: Are the plays true to history? The answer seems to be that the main outline of the story is true, but that Shakespeare had to compress events so much in order to get them into a three-hour play that inevitably there must be some distortion. Characters also are not necessarily true to their historical originals. Richard III, in particular, is much more wicked in the play than he was in life.

ROMANCES

This is the last group of Shakespeare's plays. They are sometimes called the 'tragicomedies' because they begin in a tragic vein and end up happily. It is often argued that these plays represent a change in outlook in Shakespeare himself. Written towards the end of his dramatic career, and after the tragedies, they seem to suggest a more hopeful view of life than that presented in the tragedies, where everything ends in death and disaster. In the romances, characters who have been separated through conflict and misunderstanding are finally reunited, old feuds are forgotten and a new life begins, based on forgiveness and love.

Now look at the chart giving the dates of composition and the four categories of Shakespeare's plays. When you have studied it, answer the questions on it.

PERIOD	TRAGEDIES	COMEDIES	HISTORIES	ROMANCES
1584 I	Titus Andronicus	The Comedy of Errors The Taming of the Shrew The Two Gentlemen of Verona	Henry VI, Parts 1,2,3 Richard III King John	
*1592		Love's Labour's Lost		
1594 II	Romeo and Juliet	A Midsummer Night's Dream The Merchant of Venice The Merry Wives of Windsor Much Ado About Nothing As You Like It	Richard II Henry IV, Part 1 Henry IV, Part 2 Henry V	
1599 III	Julius Caesar Hamlet, Prince of Denmark Othello, the Moor of Venice Timon of Athens King Lear Macbeth Antony and Cleopatra Coriolanus	Twelfth Night; or What You Will Troilus and Cressida Measure for Measure All's Well That Ends Well		
1608 IV 1613			 Henry VIII	Pericles, Prince of Tyre Cymbeline The Winter's Tale The Tempest

This is an approximate order of composition. We don't know the exact date when each play was written.   *1592: the year in which the first reference is made to Shakespeare in London.

CHECKPOINT

1 What do you notice about the differences of title between the comedies and the tragedies?
2 Which titles amongst the comedies lead you to expect a light-hearted, humorous play?
3 Which plays listed as comedies have titles similar to the tragedies?
4 Which tragedies would you expect to be about love?
5 From the chart, would you say that Shakespeare had periods when he wrote a certain type of play?
6 During which periods was he most active as a dramatist?
7 When did he write least?
8 What is unexpected about the order in which the histories were written?
9 How many plays did Shakespeare write? (You may include the plays, like *Titus Andronicus* and *Henry VIII*, which Shakespeare may have written in collaboration with another dramatist.)

ENTER TWO MURDERERS

from *Richard III*

Richard, Duke of Gloucester, (and eventually King Richard III) is ambitious to become king, but must first get rid of his brother, CLARENCE. He therefore imprisons Clarence in the Tower and sends two men with a commission to murder him. In this scene the murderers have a struggle with their consciences, but murder wins.

ACT 1, SCENE 4

Enter the two MURDERERS.

1 MURDERER	Ho! who's here?	5
BRAKENBURY	What wouldst thou, fellow, and how cam'st thou hither?	
1 MURDERER	I would speak with Clarence, and I came hither on my legs.	
BRAKENBURY	What, so brief?	
2 MURDERER	'Tis better, sir, than to be tedious. Let him see our commission and talk no more. [BRAKENBURY *reads it.*	10
BRAKENBURY	I am, in this, commanded to deliver The noble Duke of Clarence to your hands. I will not reason what is meant hereby, Because I will be guiltless from the meaning. There lies the Duke asleep; and there the keys. I'll to the King and signify to him That thus I have resign'd to you my charge.	15
1 MURDERER	You may, sir; 'tis a point of wisdom. Fare you well. [*Exeunt* BRAKENBURY *and* KEEPER.	
2 MURDERER	What, shall I stab him as he sleeps?	20
1 MURDERER	No; he'll say 'twas done cowardly, when he wakes.	
2 MURDERER	Why, he shall never wake until the great judgment-day.	
1 MURDERER	Why, then he'll say we stabb'd him sleeping.	
2 MURDERER	The urging of that word judgment hath bred a kind of remorse in me.	25
1 MURDERER	What, art thou afraid?	
2 MURDERER	Not to kill him, having a warrant; but to be damn'd for killing him, from the which no warrant can defend me.	
1 MURDERER	I thought thou hadst been resolute.	
2 MURDERER	So I am, to let him live.	30
1 MURDERER	I'll back to the Duke of Gloucester and tell him so.	

2 MURDERER	Nay, I prithee, stay a little. I hope this passionate humour of mine will change; it was wont to hold me but while one tells twenty.	
1 MURDERER	How dost thou feel thyself now?	35
2 MURDERER	Faith, some certain dregs of conscience are yet within me.	
1 MURDERER	Remember our reward, when the deed's done.	
2 MURDERER	Zounds, he dies; I had forgot the reward.	
1 MURDERER	Where's thy conscience now?	40
2 MURDERER	O, in the Duke of Gloucester's purse!	
1 MURDERER	When he opens his purse to give us our reward, thy conscience flies out.	
2 MURDERER	'Tis no matter; let it go; there's few or none will entertain it.	45
1 MURDERER	What if it come to thee again?	
2 MURDERER	I'll not meddle with it – it makes a man a coward: a man cannot steal, but it accuseth him; a man cannot swear, but it checks him; a man cannot lie with his neighbour's wife, but it detects him. 'Tis a blushing shamefac'd spirit that mutinies in a man's bosom; it fills a man full of obstacles: it made me once restore a purse of gold that – by chance I found. It beggars any man that keeps it. It is turn'd out of towns and cities for a dangerous thing; and every man that means to live well endeavours to trust to himself and live without it.	50 55
1 MURDERER	Zounds, 'tis even now at my elbow, persuading me not to kill the Duke.	
2 MURDERER	Take the devil in thy mind and believe him not; he would insinuate with thee but to make thee sigh.	60
1 MURDERER	I am strong-fram'd; he cannot prevail with me.	
2 MURDERER	Spoke like a tall man that respects thy reputation. Come, shall we fall to work?	
1 MURDERER	Take him on the costard with the hilts of thy sword, and then chop him in the malmsey-butt in the next room.	65
2 MURDERER	O excellent device! and make a sop of him.	
1 MURDERER	Soft! he wakes.	
2 MURDERER	Strike!	

59 *him*: i.e. conscience.

64 *costard*: a large apple, but here it means 'head'.

DRAMATIC EFFECTS

1 The situation in the scene is a tragic one (the intended murder of Clarence), but the murderers are treated as comic villains.
   * Can you give an example of a serious line followed by a comic one?

2 Drama is often built upon a feeling of 'will he – won't he?' Which part of the dialogue introduces this kind of uncertainty?

3 Shakespeare often makes a comment on life through his characters. In this extract he makes fun of the shallowness of the Second Murderer's conscience. Which lines demonstrate this? How would an audience react to them?

4 The long speech by the Second Murderer on conscience is made easier to follow by its containing several examples of the way conscience (according to the murderer) operates. Why would the example he gives of himself earn a special laugh?
   '... **it made me once restore a purse of gold that – by chance I found**.'

5 In which lines does Shakespeare make the comedy gruesome?

6 Can you quote some lines which create dramatic suspense?

GOOD KING OF CATS

from *Romeo and Juliet*

In the Italian city of Verona the Montague and Capulet families are deadly enemies, yet ROMEO, a Montague, has fallen in love with JULIET, a Capulet, and secretly married her. As he returns from the wedding ceremony, he comes upon a street fight between MERCUTIO, his close friend, and the brilliant swordsman, TYBALT, who is Juliet's cousin. Tybalt has no real quarrel with Mercutio – it is Romeo he is after and he challenges him. Romeo refuses the challenge because he no longer feels enmity towards the Capulets.

ACT 3, SCENE 1

(Benvolio and Mercutio are walking through the streets, chatting idly, when Tybalt and his friends suddenly appear.)

Enter TYBALT *and Others.*

BENVOLIO	By my head, here comes the Capulets.	35
MERCUTIO	By my heel, I care not.	
TYBALT	Follow me close, for I will speak to them.	
	Gentlemen, good den; a word with one of you.	38 *den*: evening
MERCUTIO	And but one word with one of us?	
	Couple it with something; make it a word and a blow.	40
TYBALT	You shall find me apt enough to that, sir, an you will give me occasion.	41 *an*: if 42 *occasion*: excuse
MERCUTIO	Could you not take some occasion without giving?	43 *occasion*: opportunity
TYBALT	Mercutio, thou consortest with Romeo.	44–5 *consortest with*: keep company with . . . *consort*: keep in tune with
MERCUTIO	Consort! What, dost thou make us minstrels? An thou make minstrels of us, look to hear nothing but discords. Here's my fiddlestick; here's that shall make you dance. Zounds, consort!	45

BENVOLIO	We talk here in the public haunt of men;	
	Either withdraw unto some private place,	50
	Or reason coldly of your grievances,	
	Or else depart; here all eyes gaze on us.	
MERCUTIO	Men's eyes were made to look, and let them gaze;	
	I will not budge for no man's pleasure, I.	

Enter ROMEO.

TYBALT	Well, peace be with you, sir. Here comes my man.	55
MERCUTIO	But I'll be hang'd, sir, if he wear your livery.	
	Marry, go before to field, he'll be your follower;	
	Your worship in that sense may call him man.	
TYBALT	Romeo, the love I bear thee can afford	
	No better term than this: thou art a villain.	60
ROMEO	Tybalt, the reason that I have to love thee	
	Doth much excuse the appertaining rage	
	To such a greeting. Villain am I none:	
	Therefore, farewell; I see thou knowest me not.	
TYBALT	Boy, this shall not excuse the injuries	65
	That thou hast done me; therefore turn and draw.	
ROMEO	I do protest I never injur'd thee,	
	But love thee better than thou canst devise	
	Till thou shalt know the reason of my love;	
	And so, good Capulet – which name I tender	70
	As dearly as mine own – be satisfied.	
MERCUTIO	O calm, dishonourable, vile submission!	
	Alla stoccata carries it away. *[Draws.*	
	Tybalt, you rat-catcher, will you walk?	
TYBALT	What wouldst thou have with me?	75
MERCUTIO	Good King of Cats, nothing but one of your nine lives;	
	that I mean to make bold withal, and, as you shall use	
	me hereafter, dry-beat the rest of the eight. Will you	
	pluck your sword out of his pilcher by the ears? Make	
	haste, lest mine be about your ears ere it be out.	80
TYBALT	I am for you. *[Draws.*	
ROMEO	Gentle Mercutio, put thy rapier up.	
MERCUTIO	Come, sir, your passado. *[They fight.*	
ROMEO	Draw, Benvolio; beat down their weapons.	
	Gentlemen, for shame, forbear this outrage!	85
	Tybalt! Mercutio! the Prince expressly hath	
	Forbid this bandying in Verona streets.	
	Hold, Tybalt! Good Mercutio!	

[Tybalt under Romeo's arms thrusts Mercutio in, and flies with his friends.

MERCUTIO	I am hurt.	
	A plague a both your houses! I am sped.	90
	Is he gone and hath nothing?	
BENVOLIO	What, art thou hurt?	
MERCUTIO	Ay, ay, a scratch, a scratch; marry, 'tis enough.	
	Where is my page? Go, villain, fetch a surgeon.	

[Exit PAGE.

ROMEO	Courage, man; the hurt cannot be much.	95
MERCUTIO	No, 'tis not so deep as a well, nor so wide as a church	
	door, but 'tis enough, 'twill serve. Ask for me to-morrow,	
	and you shall find me a grave man. I am peppered, I	
	warrant, for this world. A plague a both your houses!	
	Zounds, a dog, a rat, a mouse, a cat, to scratch a man to	100
	death! A braggart, a rogue, a villain, that fights by the	
	book of arithmetic! Why the devil came you between us?	
	I was hurt under your arm.	

52 *depart*: separate

55 *my man*: Tybalt means 'the man I want', but Mercutio takes it to mean 'my servant'

62 *appertaining*: appropriate

70 *tender*: care for.

73 *Alla stoccata*: a sword-thrust (referring to Tybalt's aggressiveness).

77 *withal*: with.
78 *dry-beat*: beat soundly.
79 *his pilcher*: his scabbard.

83 *passado*: forward thrust with sword.

87 *bandying*: fighting.

94 *villain*: servant

98 *peppered*: done for

102 *the book of arithmetic*: by numbers, according to theory

ROMEO	I thought all for the best.	
MERCUTIO	Help me into some house, Benvolio, or I shall faint	105
	A plague a both your houses!	
	They have made worms' meat of me.	
	I have it, and soundly too – Your houses!	

[Exeunt MERCUTIO *and* BENVOLIO.

ROMEO	This gentleman, the Prince's near ally,	
	My very friend, hath got this mortal hurt	110
	In my behalf; my reputation stain'd	
	With Tybalt's slander – Tybalt, that an hour	
	Hath been my cousin. O sweet Juliet,	
	Thy beauty hath made me effeminate,	
	And in my temper soft'ned valour's steel!	115

Re-enter BENVOLIO.

BENVOLIO	O Romeo, Romeo, brave Mercutio is dead!	
	That gallant spirit hath aspir'd the clouds,	
	Which too untimely here did scorn the earth.	
ROMEO	This day's black fate on moe days doth depend;	
	This but begins the woe others must end.	120

Re-enter TYBALT.

BENVOLIO	Here comes the furious Tybalt back again.	
ROMEO	Alive in triumph and Mercutio slain!	
	Away to heaven respective lenity,	
	And fire-ey'd fury be my conduct now!	
	Now, Tybalt, take the 'villain' back again	125
	That late thou gav'st me; for Mercutio's soul	
	Is but a little way above our heads,	
	Staying for thine to keep him company.	
	Either thou or I, or both, must go with him.	
TYBALT	Thou, wretched boy, that didst consort him here,	130
	Shalt with him hence.	
ROMEO	This shall determine that.	

[They fight; TYBALT *falls.*

BENVOLIO	Romeo, away, be gone.	
	The citizens are up, and Tybalt slain.	
	Stand not amaz'd. The Prince will doom thee death	135
	If thou art taken. Hence, be gone, away!	
ROMEO	O, I am fortune's fool.	
BENVOLIO	Why dost thou stay?	

[Exit ROMEO.

Enter CITIZENS.

FIRST CITIZEN	Which way ran he that kill'd Mercutio?	
	Tybalt, that murderer, which way ran he?	140
BENVOLIO	There lies that Tybalt.	
FIRST CITIZEN	Up, sir, go with me;	
	I charge thee in the Prince's name, obey.	

Enter PRINCE, *attended;* MONTAGUE, CAPULET, *their Wives, and All.*

PRINCE	Where are the vile beginners of this fray?	

123 *respective lenity*: being lenient towards Tybalt
125 *take the villain back*: take back the word 'villain'

137 *fortune's fool*: a prey to fortune

When you study a complete Shakespeare play, you will probably have to write about the characters in it. In order to give you some help with this kind of study, we shall look closely at the character of Mercutio in the extract you have just read. We'll get to know him by noting what he does, what he says, and what other people say about him. We'll play the game of liking or disliking him as though he were a real person. The first step is to follow the scene through and make some notes:

NOTES ON MERCUTIO

- he doesn't care that the Capulets are coming;
- he seems to want to pick a quarrel with Tybalt when he says:

  And but one word with one of us?
  Couple it with something; make it a
  word and a blow.

- he enjoys playing with words – making puns, twisting them to give a different meaning – e.g. 'occasion', 'consort', 'man' – usually an insulting one;
- because he wants a quarrel, he stubbornly refuses to follow Benvolio's suggestion and go to a more private place – or at least to talk reasonably;
- he is furious when Romeo refuses to take up Tybalt's challenge:

  O calm, dishonourable, vile submission!
  and draws his sword to fight Tybalt himself. Is he just hot-headed, or has he a real sense of honour?

- he is probably no match for Tybalt, yet he is aggressive and over-confident:

  Good King of Cats, nothing but one of
  your nine lives ...
  ... Make haste ...

- when he is hurt, he turns on both the houses – Montague and Capulet – as if they were to blame;
- even when he is dying, he cannot resist a bitter joke:

  Ask for me to-morrow, and you shall
  find me a grave man.

- he implies that Tybalt somehow fought unfairly by scratching him with his sword ('a braggart, a rogue, a villain') and he blames Romeo for coming between them and allowing Tybalt an advantage;
- he seems bewildered and outraged that the feuding houses should have been the cause of his death – of making 'worms' meat' out of him.

Your notes can then be used to sum up Mercutio's character:

> Mercutio is emotional and hot-headed, easily drawn into a fight on the slightest excuse. He cannot resist making witty replies to Tybalt's remarks and deliberately twists Tybalt's words so that they appear to be insults. His fiery temper flares up at what he thinks is a cowardly submission by Romeo and he takes up the challenge himself. Tybalt is obviously the better swordsman, yet Mercutio is full of boasts and wild threats. When he is slain, his wit remains brilliant, but bitter: 'Ask for me to-morrow, and you shall find me a grave man. I am peppered, I warrant, for this world.' He never admits that he is to blame, but curses the two feuding families for being the cause of the fight and Romeo for intervening and giving Tybalt an opportunity to strike. Yet for all his faults, Mercutio is a likeable character whose tragic death is more moving because he has seemed so convincingly human.

* Following the method used for the study of Mercutio, write detailed notes and then a final character sketch for:

  a Romeo   **b** Tybalt.

HOTSPUR AND THE POPINJAY

from *Henry IV, Part 1*

Hotspur fought for King Henry and took some prisoners in battle. A lord – fashionably dressed, smelling of perfume – arrives on the battlefield and asks Hotspur to hand over the prisoners for the king. Hotspur – faint and exhausted – from the fighting – is annoyed by this effeminate lord and refuses to hand over the prisoners. Later, at the court of King Henry, Hotspur explains his annoyance.

ACT 1, SCENE 3

HOTSPUR	My liege, I did deny no prisoners.
	But I remember when the fight was done,
	When I was dry with rage and extreme toil,
	Breathless and faint, leaning upon my sword,
	Came there a certain lord, neat, and trimly dress'd, 5
	Fresh as a bridegroom, and his chin new reap'd
	Show'd like a stubble-land at harvest-home;
	He was perfumed like a milliner,
	And 'twixt his finger and his thumb he held
	A pouncet-box, which ever and anon 10
	He gave his nose and took't away again;
	Who therewith angry, when it next came there,
	Took it in snuff – and still he smil'd and talk'd –
	And as the soldiers bore dead bodies by,
	He call'd them untaught knaves, unmannerly, 15
	To bring a slovenly unhandsome corse
	Betwixt the wind and his nobility.
	With many holiday and lady terms
	He questioned me: amongst the rest, demanded
	My prisoners in your Majesty's behalf. 20
	I then, all smarting with my wounds being cold,
	To be so pest'red with a popinjay,
	Out of my grief and my impatience
	Answer'd neglectingly I know not what –
	He should, or he should not – for he made me mad 25
	To see him shine so brisk, and smell so sweet,
	And talk so like a waiting-gentlewoman
	Of guns, and drums, and wounds – God save the mark! –
	And telling me the sovereignest thing on earth
	Was parmaceti for an inward bruise; 30
	And that it was great pity, so it was,
	This villainous saltpetre should be digg'd
	Out of the bowels of the harmless earth,
	Which many a good tall fellow had destroy'd
	So cowardly; and but for these vile guns 35
	He would himself have been a soldier.
	This bald unjointed chat of his, my lord,
	I answered indirectly, as I said;
	And I beseech you, let not his report
	Come current for an accusation 40
	Betwixt my love and your high Majesty.

1 *liege*: lord

10 *pouncet-pox*: small box for perfumes

16 *corse*: corpse

18 *holiday and lady terms*: dainty and feminine expressions

22 *popinjay*: parrot

29 *sovereignest thing*: best remedy
30 *parmaceti*: a version of 'spermaceti', oil from the sperm whale
32 *saltpetre*: potassium nitrate, used in making gunpowder

40 *come current*: be considered true

Hotspur's speech is a good example of Shakespeare's power to describe character and situation in vivid, concrete language.

1 Quote the lines that give a striking picture of Hotspur after the battle.

2 In describing the 'certain lord', Hotspur uses four similes. Identify them and make a comment on any one of them, saying how appropriate it is to convey Hotspur's feelings about the lord.

3 In which lines would Hotspur probably mimic the speech and manner of the lord?

4 Expressing his own feelings, Hotspur's language is very down-to-earth. Can you quote some examples?

5 Write a brief account of Hotspur's speech, using appropriate quotations.

ALL HONOURABLE MEN

from *Julius Caesar*

JULIUS CAESAR has been assassinated on the steps of the Capitol in Rome by a group of conspirators, led by CASSIUS and BRUTUS. Cassius is envious of Caesar's power; Brutus fears that Rome will suffer if this power increases.

MARK ANTONY, a friend of Caesar's, is shocked by the killing, but he dare not openly oppose the assassins for fear of his own life. Instead, he asks permission of Brutus to make a funeral speech to the Roman citizens over the body of Caesar. Brutus agrees; but Antony is allowed to speak only after Brutus has given his reasons to the people for joining in the conspiracy to kill Caesar.

ACT 3, SCENE 2

ROME. THE FORUM

Enter BRUTUS *and* CASSIUS *with the* PLEBEIANS.

CITIZENS We will be satisfied! Let us be satisfied!

BRUTUS Then follow me, and give me audience, friends.
Cassius, go you into the other street,
And part the numbers.   4 *part*: divide
Those that will hear me speak, let 'em stay here;   5
Those that will follow Cassius, go with him;
And public reasons shall be rendered
Of Caesar's death.

FIRST PLEBEIAN   I will hear Brutus speak.

SECOND PLEBEIAN I will hear Cassius, and compare their reasons,   10
When severally we hear them rendered.
                    [*Exit* CASSIUS, *with some of the* PLEBEIANS.
                 BRUTUS *goes into the pulpit.*

THIRD PLEBEIAN The noble Brutus is ascended. Silence!

BRUTUS Be patient till the last.
Romans, countrymen, and lovers! hear me for my
cause, and be silent, that you may hear. Believe me for   15
mine honour, and have respect to mine honour, that
you may believe. Censure me in your wisdom, and   17 *censure*: blame
awake your senses, that you may the better judge. If

there be any in this assembly, any dear friend of
Caesar's, to him I say that Brutus' love to Caesar was   20
no less than his. If then that friend demand why
Brutus rose against Caesar, this is my answer: Not
that I lov'd Caesar less, but that I lov'd Rome more.
Had you rather Caesar were living, and die all slaves,
than that Caesar were dead, to live all free men? As   25
Caesar lov'd me, I weep for him; as he was fortunate, I
rejoice at it; as he was valiant, I honour him; but – as
he was ambitious, I slew him. There is tears for his
love; joy for his fortune; honour for his valour; and
death for his ambition. Who is here so base that would   30
be a bondman? If any, speak; for him have I offended.
Who is here so rude that would not be a Roman? If any,
speak; for him have I offended. Who is here so vile that
will not love his country? If any, speak; for him have I
offended. I pause for a reply.   35

ALL   None, Brutus, none.
BRUTUS   Then none have I offended. I have done no more to
Caesar than you shall do to Brutus. The question of his
death is enroll'd in the Capitol; his glory not
extenuated, wherein he was worthy; nor his offences   40
enforc'd, for which he suffered death.

Enter MARK ANTONY *and* OTHERS *with Caesar's body.*

Here comes his body, mourn'd by Mark Antony, who,
though he had no hand in his death, shall receive the
benefit of his dying, a place in the commonwealth, as
which of you shall not? With this I depart, that, as I   45
slew my best lover for the good of Rome, I have the same
dagger for myself, when it shall please my country to
need my death.

ALL   Live, Brutus! live, live!
FIRST PLEBEIAN   Bring him with triumph home unto his house.   50
SECOND PLEBEIAN   Give him a statue with his ancestors.
THIRD PLEBEIAN   Let him be Caesar.
FOURTH PLEBEIAN   Caesar's better parts
Shall be crown'd in Brutus.
FIRST PLEBEIAN   We'll bring him to his house with shouts and clamours.   55
BRUTUS   My countrymen –
SECOND PLEBEIAN   Peace, silence! Brutus speaks.
FIRST PLEBEIAN   Peace, ho!
BRUTUS   Good countrymen, let me depart alone,
And for my sake stay here with Antony.   60
Do grace to Caesar's corpse, and grace his speech
Tending to Caesar's glories, which Mark Antony
By our permission, is allow'd to make.
I do entreat you, not a man depart
Save I alone, till Antony have spoke.   *[Exit.* 65
FIRST PLEBEIAN   Stay, ho! and let us hear Mark Antony.
THIRD PLEBEIAN   Let him go up into the public chair.
We'll hear him. Noble Antony, go up.
ANTONY   For Brutus' sake I am beholding to you. *[Goes up.*
FOURTH PLEBEIAN   What does he say of Brutus?   70
THIRD PLEBEIAN   He says, for Brutus' sake
He finds himself beholding to us all.
FOURTH PLEBEIAN   'Twere best he speak no harm of Brutus here.
FIRST PLEBEIAN   This Caesar was a tyrant.

30 *base*: low, despicable
31 *bondman*: slave
32 *rude*: barbarous

39 *enroll'd*: written on a roll of parchment
40 *extenuated*: lessened
41 *enforc'd*: emphasised

61 *Do grace to*: respect, honour

69 *beholding*: beholden, indebted

85

THIRD PLEBEIAN	Nay, that's certain.	75
	We are blest that Rome is rid of him.	
SECOND PLEBEIAN	Peace! let us hear what Antony can say.	
ANTONY	You gentle Romans —	
ALL	Peace, ho! let us hear him.	
ANTONY	Friends, Romans, countrymen, lend me your ears;	80

ANTONY   Friends, Romans, countrymen, lend me your ears;   80
I come to bury Caesar, not to praise him.
The evil that men do lives after them;
The good is oft interred with their bones;
So let it be with Caesar. The noble **Brutus**
Hath told you Caesar was ambitious.   85
If it were so, it was a grievous fault;
And grievously hath Caesar answer'd it.
Here, under leave of Brutus and the **rest** —
For Brutus is an honourable man;
So are they all, all honourable men —   90
Come I to speak in Caesar's funeral.
He was my friend, faithful and just **to me**;
But Brutus says he was ambitious,
And Brutus is an honourable man.
He hath brought many captives home to Rome,   95
Whose ransoms did the general coffers fill;
Did this in Caesar seem ambitious?
When that the poor have cried, Caesar hath wept;
Ambition should be made of sterner stuff.
Yet Brutus says he was ambitious;   100
And Brutus is an honourable man.
You all did see that on the Lupercal
I thrice presented him a kingly crown,
Which he did thrice refuse. Was this ambition?
Yet Brutus says he was ambitious;   105
And sure he is an honourable man.
I speak not to disprove what Brutus spoke,
But here I am to speak what I do know.
You all did love him once, not without cause;
What cause witholds you, then, to mourn for him?   110
O judgment, thou art fled to brutish beasts,
And men have lost their reason! Bear with me;
My heart is in the coffin there with Caesar,
And I must pause till it come back to me.

FIRST PLEBEIAN   Methinks there is much reason in his sayings.   115
SECOND PLEBEIAN   If thou consider rightly of the matter,
Caesar has had great wrong.
THIRD PLEBEIAN   Has he, masters!
I fear there will a worse come in his place.
FOURTH PLEBEIAN   Mark'd ye his words? He would not take the crown;   120
Therefore 'tis certain he was not ambitious.
FIRST PLEBEIAN   If it be found so, some will dear abide it.
SECOND PLEBEIAN   Poor soul! his eyes are red as fire with weeping.
THIRD PLEBEIAN   There's not a nobler man in Rome than Antony.
FOURTH PLEBEIAN   Now mark him, he begins again to speak.   125
ANTONY   But yesterday the word of Caesar might
Have stood against the world: now lies he there,
And none so poor to do him reverence.
O masters, if I were dispos'd to stir
Your hearts and minds to mutiny and rage,   130
I should do Brutus wrong, and Cassius wrong,
Who, you all know, are honourable men.
I will not do them wrong; I rather choose
To wrong the dead, to wrong myself and you,
Than I will wrong such honourable men.   135

83 *interred*: buried

96 *the general coffers*:
the public treasury

102 *Lupercal*: Roman
festival of
Lupercus (Pan)

111 *judgment*:
discretion

122 *dear abide it*: pay
dearly for it

	But here's a parchment with the seal of Caesar,
	I found it in his closet – 'tis his will.
	Let but the commons hear this testament,
	Which, pardon me, I do not mean to read,
	And they would go and kiss dead Caesar's wounds 140
	And dip their napkins in his sacred blood;
	Yea, beg a hair of him for memory
	And, dying, mention it within their wills,
	Bequeathing it as a rich legacy
	Unto their issue. 145
FOURTH PLEBEIAN	We'll hear the will. Read it, Mark Antony.
ALL	The will, the will! We will hear Caesar's will.
ANTONY	Have patience, gentle friends, I must not read it;
	It is not meet you know how Caesar lov'd you.
	You are not wood, you are not stones, but men; 150
	And being men, hearing the will of Caesar,
	It will inflame you, it will make you mad.
	'Tis good you know not that you are his heirs;
	For if you should, O, what would come of it?
FOURTH PLEBEIAN	Read the will; we'll hear it, Antony! 155
	You shall read us the will – Caesar's will.
ANTONY	Will you be patient? Will you stay awhile?
	I have o'ershot myself to tell you of it.
	I fear I wrong the honourable men
	Whose daggers have stabb'd Caesar; I do fear it. 160
FOURTH PLEBEIAN	They were traitors. Honourable men!
ALL	The will! the testament!
SECOND PLEBEIAN	They were villains, murderers. The will! Read the will.
ANTONY	You will compel me, then, to read the will?
	Then make a ring about the corpse of Caesar, 165
	And let me show you him that made the will.
	Shall I descend? and will you give me leave?
ALL	Come down.
SECOND PLEBEIAN	Descend. [ANTONY *comes down.*
THIRD PLEBEIAN	You shall have leave. 170
FOURTH PLEBEIAN	A ring! Stand round.
FIRST PLEBEIAN	Stand from the hearse, stand from the body.
SECOND PLEBEIAN	Room for Antony, most noble Antony!
ANTONY	Nay, press not so upon me; stand far off.
ALL	Stand back. Room! Bear back. 175
ANTONY	If you have tears, prepare to shed them now.
	You all do know this mantle. I remember
	The first time ever Caesar put it on;
	'Twas on a summer's evening, in his tent,
	That day he overcame the Nervii. 180
	Look! in this place ran Cassius' dagger through;
	See what a rent the envious Casca made;
	Through this the well-beloved Brutus stabb'd,
	And as he pluck'd his cursed steel away,
	Mark how the blood of Caesar follow'd it, 185
	As rushing out of doors, to be resolv'd
	If Brutus so unkindly knock'd or no;
	For Brutus, as you know, was Caesar's angel.
	Judge, O you gods, how dearly Caesar lov'd him!
	This was the most unkindest cut of all; 190
	For when the noble Caesar saw him stab,
	Ingratitude, more strong than traitors' arms,
	Quite vanquish'd him. Then burst his mighty heart;
	And in his mantle muffling up his face,
	Even at the base of Pompey's statua, 195

Glossary / notes (right margin):

138 *commons*: common people

141 *napkins*: handkerchiefs

149 *meet*: appropriate

158 *o'ershot myself*: gone too far

177 *mantle*: cloak

186 *to be resolv'd*: to decide

	Which all the while ran blood, great Caesar fell.	
	O, what a fall was there, my countrymen!	
	Then I, and you, and all of us fell down,	
	Whilst bloody treason flourish'd over us.	
	O, now you weep, and I perceive you feel	200
	The dint of pity. These are gracious drops.	
	Kind souls, what weep you when you but behold	
	Our Caesar's vesture wounded? Look you here,	
	Here is himself, marr'd as you see with traitors.	
FIRST PLEBEIAN	O piteous spectacle!	205
SECOND PLEBEIAN	O noble Caesar!	
THIRD PLEBEIAN	O woeful day!	
FOURTH PLEBEIAN	O traitors, villains!	
FIRST PLEBEIAN	O most bloody sight!	
SECOND PLEBEIAN	We will be reveng'd.	210
ALL	Revenge! About! Seek! Burn! Fire! Kill! Slay!	
	Let not a traitor live!	
ANTONY	Stay, countrymen.	
FIRST PLEBEIAN	Peace there! Here the noble Antony.	
SECOND PLEBEIAN	We'll hear him, we'll follow him, we'll die with him.	215
ANTONY	Good friends, sweet friends, let me not stir you up	
	To such a sudden flood of mutiny.	
	They that have done this deed are honourable.	
	What private griefs they have, alas, I know not,	
	That made them do it; they are wise and honourable,	220
	And will, no doubt, with reasons answer you.	
	I come not, friends to steal away your hearts;	
	I am no orator, as Brutus is,	
	But, as you know me all, a plain blunt man,	
	That love my friend; and that they know full well	225
	That gave me public leave to speak of him.	
	For I have neither wit, nor words, nor worth,	
	Action, nor utterance, nor the power of speech,	
	To stir men's blood! I only speak right on.	
	I tell you that which you yourselves do know;	230
	Show you sweet Caesar's wounds, poor poor dumb mouths.	
	And bid them speak for me. But were I Brutus,	
	And Brutus Antony, there were an Antony	
	Would ruffle up your spirits, and put a tongue	235
	In every wound of Caesar, that should move	
	The stones of Rome to rise and mutiny.	
ALL	We'll mutiny.	
FIRST PLEBEIAN	We'll burn the house of Brutus.	
THIRD PLEBEIAN	Away, then! Come seek the conspirators.	240
ANTONY	Yet hear me, countrymen; yet hear me speak.	
ALL	Peace, ho! Hear Antony, most noble Antony.	
ANTONY	Why, friends, you go to do you know not what.	
	Wherein, hath Caesar thus deserv'd your loves?	
	Alas, you know not! I must tell you, then:	245
	You have forgot the will I told you of.	
ALL	Most true. The will! Let's stay and hear the will.	
ANTONY	Here is the will, and under Caesar's seal:	
	To every Roman citizen he gives,	
	To every several man, seventy-five drachmas.	250
SECOND PLEBEIAN	Most noble Caesar! We'll revenge his death.	
THIRD PLEBEIAN	O royal Caesar!	
ANTONY	Hear me with patience.	
ALL	Peace, ho!	

201 *dint*: force

203 *vesture*: garment

211 *About*: set about it!

219 *griefs*: grievances

250 *every several man*: each individual
250 *drachmas*: ancient Greek silver coins

ANTONY	Moreover, he hath left you all his walks,	255
	His private arbours, and new-planted orchards,	
	On this side Tiber; he hath left them you,	
	And to your heirs for ever — common pleasures,	
	To walk abroad and recreate yourselves.	
	Here was a Caesar! When comes such another?	260
FIRST PLEBEIAN	Never, never! Come away, away!	
	We'll burn his body in the holy place,	
	And with the brands fire the traitors' houses.	
	Take up the body.	
SECOND PLEBEIAN	Go, fetch fire.	265
THIRD PLEBEIAN	Pluck down benches.	
FOURTH PLEBEIAN	Pluck down forms, windows, any thing.	
	[*Exeunt* PLEBEIANS *with the body.*	
ANTONY	Now let it work. Mischief, thou art afoot,	
	Take thou what course thou wilt.	

Glossary:
256 *arbours*: shady retreats
259 *recreate yourselves*: enjoy recreation
263 *brands*: burning pieces of wood

POLITICAL DRAMA

This scene is an example of Shakespeare's skill at dramatising public events, even though the crowds of Rome are represented by a mere handful of actors playing the citizens.

The drama is created by the powerful speeches of Brutus and Antony and the effect these speeches have upon the citizens of Rome. The following questions will help you to study these two dramatic elements in the scene.

THE CITIZENS

At the beginning of the scene the citizens love Brutus; at the end they condemn him as a traitor. Trace the changing mood of the citizens by summarising what they say in the following groups of lines:

i   The entry of Cassius and Brutus: 1–11
    *The citizens are prepared
    to listen to the arguments
    of the conspirators and to
    judge them fairly.*

ii   After Brutus's first speech: 49–58; 66–79
    (**Be patient till the last**)

iii   After Antony's first speech: 115–125
    (**Friends, Romans,
    countrymen . . .**)

iv   After Antony's second speech: 146–175
    (**But yesterday the word of
    Caesar . . .**)

v   After Antony's third speech: 205–215
    (**If you have tears . . .**)

vi   After Antony's fourth speech: 238–242;
    (**Good friends, sweet friends . . .**) 251–254
    261–267

MARK ANTONY

Antony's clever oratory deceives the citizens, but not the audience (or the reader). It is another example of Shakespeare's irony that we see through Antony's technique of rousing the citizens to rebellion, but they themselves are unaware of it. Let us look more closely at this technique.

1 a   In the first speech (lines 80–114), what examples does Antony give to prove that Caesar was *not* ambitious?
  b   Why does he repeat the phrase 'honourable man' so much?
  c   In which lines would Antony appear to be overcome with emotion for the dead Caesar?

2   Study Antony's technique in referring to the will of Caesar and eventually reading it.

3   Study Antony's third speech (lines 176–204) and explain exactly what he is doing during the speech and particularly in lines 195–6.

4   Quote some of the things Antony says about himself in his fourth speech (lines 216–237). Can you explain what dramatic effect Shakespeare is creating here?

5   What are we to understand about Antony from his final remark? (lines 268–9)

SUMMING UP

Using the answers you have made to the questions on the citizens and on Mark Antony, write two short paragraphs on the dramatic qualities of this scene from *Julius Caesar*.

DOWN IN THE FOREST

from *As You Like It*

Rosalind fell in love with Orlando when she saw him wrestling and gave him a chain from her neck as a hint of her affection. Orlando fell in love with her, though they exchanged only a few words.

Independently of each other, they flee to the Forest of Arden to escape the tyranny of the usurping Duke Frederick. Rosalind disguises herself as a boy and is accompanied by her cousin Celia.

In this scene, Rosalind has just found a love poem pinned to a tree. Celia saw that it was Orlando who put it there, but she teases Rosalind by refusing to tell her who it was.

ACT 3, SCENE 2

ROSALIND	Good my complexion! dost thou think, though I am caparison'd like a man, I have a doublet and hose in my disposition? One inch of delay more is a South Sea of discovery. I prithee tell me who is it quickly, and speak apace. I would thou could'st stammer, that thou mighst pour this conceal'd man out of thy mouth, as wine comes out of a narrow-mouth'd bottle – either too much at once or none at all. I prithee take the cork out of thy mouth that I may drink thy tidings.	190

195 |
CELIA	So you may put a man in your belly.	
ROSALIND	Is he of God's making? What manner of man? Is his head worth a hat or his chin worth a beard?	200
CELIA	Nay, he hath but a little beard.	
ROSALIND	Why, God will send more if the man will be thankful. Let me stay the growth of his beard, if thou delay me not the knowledge of his chin.	205
CELIA	It is young Orlando, that tripp'd up the wrestler's heels and your heart both in an instant.	
ROSALIND	Nay, but the devil take mocking! Speak sad brow and true maid.	
CELIA	I' faith, coz, 'tis he.	210
ROSALIND	Orlando?	
CELIA	Orlando.	
ROSALIND	Alas the day! what shall I do with my doublet and hose? What did he when thou saw'st him? What said he? How look'd he? Wherein went he? What makes he here? Did he ask for me? Where remains he? How parted he with thee? And when shalt thou see him again? Answer me in one word.	215
CELIA	You must borrow me Gargantua's mouth first; 'tis a word too great for any mouth of this age's size. To say ay and no to these particulars is more than to answer in a catechism.	220
ROSALIND	But doth he know that I am in this forest, and in man's apparel? Looks he as freshly as he did the day he wrestled?	225
CELIA	It is as easy to count atomies as to resolve the propositions of a lover; but take a taste of my finding him, and relish it with good observance. I found him under a tree, like a dropp'd acorn.	

191 *caparison'd*: dressed
191–2 *doublet and hose in my disposition*: a man's character

204 *stay*: wait for

210 *coz*: cousin

215 *wherein*: in what clothes
215 *what makes he*: what does he do

219 *Gargantua*: a giant

226 *atomies*: atoms, motes
227 *propositions*: questions

ROSALIND	It may well be call'd Jove's tree, when it drops forth such fruit.	230
CELIA	Give me audience, good madam.	
ROSALIND	Proceed.	
CELIA	There lay he, stretch'd along like a wounded knight.	
ROSALIND	Though it be pity to see such a sight, it well becomes the ground.	235
CELIA	Cry "Holla" to thy tongue, I prithee; it curvets unseasonably. He was furnish'd like a hunter.	
ROSALIND	O, ominous! he comes to kill my heart.	
CELIA	I would sing my song without a burden; thou bring'st me out of tune.	240
ROSALIND	Do you not know I am a woman? When I think, I must speak. Sweet, say on.	
CELIA	You bring me out. Soft! comes he not here?	

Enter ORLANDO and JAQUES.

ROSALIND	'Tis he; slink by, and note him.	245
JAQUES	I thank you for your company; but, good faith, I had as lief have been myself alone.	
ORLANDO	And so had I; but yet, for fashion sake, I thank you too for your society.	
JAQUES	God buy you; let's meet as little as we can.	250
ORLANDO	I do desire we may be better strangers.	
JAQUES	I pray you mar no more trees with writing love songs in their barks.	
ORLANDO	I pray you mar no moe of my verses with reading them ill-favouredly.	255
JAQUES	Rosalind is your love's name?	
ORLANDO	Yes, just.	
JAQUES	I do not like her name.	
ORLANDO	There was no thought of pleasing you when she was christen'd.	260
JAQUES	What stature is she of?	
ORLANDO	Just as high as my heart.	
JAQUES	You are full of pretty answers. Have you not been acquainted with goldsmiths' wives, and conn'd them out of rings?	265
ORLANDO	Not so; but I answer you right painted cloth, from whence you have studied your questions.	266
JAQUES	You have a nimble wit; I think 'twas made of Atalanta's heels. Will you sit down with me? and we two will rail against our mistress the world, and all our misery.	270
ORLANDO	I will chide no breather in the world but myself, against whom I know most faults.	
JAQUES	The worst fault you have is to be in love.	
ORLANDO	'Tis a fault I will not change for your best virtue. I am weary of you.	275
JAQUES	By my troth, I was seeking for a fool when I found you.	
ORLANDO	He is drown'd in the brook; look but in, and you shall see him.	
JAQUES	There I shall see mine own figure.	
ORLANDO	Which I take to be either a fool or a cipher.	280
JAQUES	I'll tarry no longer with you; farewell, good Signior Love.	

Marginal glosses:

237 *holla*: stop!
237 *curvets*: leaps.
240 *burden*: bass accompaniment.
244 *soft*: stop, wait.
246 *I had as lief*: I would rather.
250 *God buy you*: good-bye.
257 *just*: exactly.
264 *conn'd*: learned.
266 *right painted cloth*: very briefly.
268 *Atalanta*: a swift-footed goddess.
271 *chide*: scold.
280 *cipher*: zero, a nobody.

ORLANDO	I am glad of your departure; adieu, good Monsieur Melancholy. *[Exit Jaques.*	
ROSALIND	*[Aside to Celia.]* I will speak to him like a saucy lackey, and under that habit play the knave with him. – Do you hear, forester?	285
ORLANDO	Very well; what would you?	
ROSALIND	I pray you, what is 't o'clock?	
ORLANDO	You should ask me what time o' day; there's no clock in the forest.	290
ROSALIND	Then there is no true lover in the forest, else sighing every minute and groaning every hour would detect the lazy foot of Time as well as a clock.	
ORLANDO	And why not the swift foot of Time? Had not that been as proper?	295
ROSALIND	By no means, sir. Time travels in divers paces with divers persons. I'll tell you who Time ambles withal, who Time trots withal, who Time gallops withal, and who he stands still withal.	300
ORLANDO	I prithee, who doth he trot withal?	
ROSALIND	Marry, he trots hard with a young maid between the contract of her marriage and the day it is solemnised; if the interim be but a se'nnight, Time's pace is so hard that it seems the length of seven year.	305
ORLANDO	Who ambles Time withal?	
ROSALIND	With a priest that lacks Latin and a rich man that hath not the gout; for the one sleeps easily because he cannot study, and the other lives merrily because he feels no pain the one lacking the burden of lean and wasteful learning, the other knowing no burden of heavy tedious penury. These Time ambles withal.	310
ORLANDO	Who doth he gallop withal?	
ROSALIND	With a thief to the gallows; for though he go as softly as foot can fall, he thinks himself too soon there.	315
ORLANDO	Who stays it still withal?	
ROSALIND	With lawyers in the vacation; for they sleep between term and term, and then they perceive not how Time moves.	
ORLANDO	Where dwell you, pretty youth?	320
ROSALIND	With this shepherdess, my sister; here in the skirts of the forest, like fringe upon a petticoat.	
ORLANDO	Are you native of this place?	
ROSALIND	As the coney that you see dwell where she is kindled.	
ORLANDO	Your accent is something finer than you could purchase in so removed a dwelling.	325
ROSALIND	I have been told so of many; but indeed an old religious uncle of mine taught me to speak, who was in his youth an inland man; one that knew courtship too well, for there he fell in love. I have heard him read many lectures against it; and I thank God I am not a woman, to be touch'd with so many giddy offences as he hath generally tax'd their whole sex withal.	330
ORLANDO	Can you remember any of the principal evils that he laid to the charge of women?	335
ROSALIND	There were none principal; they were all like one another as halfpence are; every one fault seeming monstrous till his fellow-fault came to match it.	
ORLANDO	I prithee recount some of them.	
ROSALIND	No; I will not cast away my physic but on those that are	340

Glossary (right margin):

285 *lackey*: man-servant.

297 *divers*: different.
298 *withal*: with.

304 *se'nnight*: seven-night (week).

312 *penury*: poverty.

324 *coney*: rabbit.
325 *purchase*: acquire.

329 *inland*: dwelling near a city.

333 *tax'd*: accused.

340 *physic*: the art of healing.

sick. There is a man haunts the forest that abuses our young plants with carving "Rosalind" on their barks; hangs odes upon hawthorns and elegies on brambles; all, forsooth, deifying the name of Rosalind. If I could meet that fancy-monger, I would give him some good 345 counsel, for he seems to have the quotidian of love upon him.

ORLANDO I am he that is so love-shak'd; I pray you tell me your remedy.

ROSALIND There is none of my uncle's marks upon you; he taught me how to know a man in love; in which cage of rushes I 350 am sure you are not prisoner.

ORLANDO What were his marks?

ROSALIND A lean cheek, which you have not; a blue eye and sunken, which you have not; an unquestionable spirit, which you have not; a beard neglected, which you have 355 not; but I pardon you for that, for simply your having in beard is a younger brother's revenue. Then your hose should be ungarter'd, your bonnet unbanded, your sleeve unbutton'd, your shoe untied, and every thing about you demonstrating a careless desolation. 360 But you are no such man; you are rather point-device in your accoutrements, as loving yourself than seeming the lover of any other.

ORLANDO Fair youth, I would I could make thee believe I love.

ROSALIND Me believe it! You may as soon make her that you love 365 believe it; which, I warrant, she is apter to do than to confess she does. That is one of the points in the which women still give the lie to their consciences. But, in good sooth, are you he that hangs the verses on the trees wherein Rosalind is so admired? 370

ORLANDO I swear to thee, youth, by the white hand of Rosalind, I am that he, that unfortunate he.

ROSALIND But are you so much in love as your rhymes speak?

ORLANDO Neither rhyme nor reason can express how much.

ROSALIND Love is merely a madness; and, I tell you, deserves 375 as well a dark house and a whip as madmen do; and the reason why they are not so punish'd and cured is that the lunacy is so ordinary that the whippers are in love too. Yet I profess curing it by counsel.

ORLANDO Did you ever cure any so? 380

ROSALIND Yes, one; and in this manner. He was to imagine me his love, his mistress; and I set him every day to woo me; at which time would I being but a moonish youth, grieve, be effeminate, changeable, longing and liking, proud, fantastical, apish, shallow, inconstant, full of 385 tears, full of smiles; for every passion something and for no passion truly anything, as boys and women are for the most part cattle of this colour; would now like him, now loathe him; then entertain him, then forswear him; now weep for him, then spit at him; that 390 I drave my suitor from his mad humour of love to a living humour of madness; which was, to forswear the full stream of the world and to live in a nook merely monastic. And thus I cur'd him; and this way will I take upon me to wash your liver as clean as a sound 395 sheep's heart, that there shall not be one spot of love in 't.

ORLANDO I would not be cured, youth.

346 *quotidian*: daily effect.

356 *your having in beard*: the amount of beard you have.
357 *a younger brother's revenue*: a small allowance.
361 *point-device*: very neat, precise.
362 *accoutrements*: equipment, outfit.

368 *give the lie to*: deceive.

388 *cattle of this colour*: people of this type.
390 *forswear*: refuse, deny.

ROSALIND	I would cure you, if you would but call me Rosalind, and come every day to my cote and woo me.	400
ORLANDO	Now, by the faith of my love, I will. Tell me where it is.	
ROSALIND	Go with me to it, and I'll show it you; and, by the way, you shall tell me where in the forest you live. Will you go?	
ORLANDO	With all my heart, good youth.	405
ROSALIND	Nay, you must call me Rosalind. Come, sister, will you go? *[Exeunt.*	

400 *cote*: cottage.

COMEDY AND ROMANCE

Many of Shakespeare's most popular plays combine romantic love with comedy and in *As You Like It* in particular, though the heroine is in love, she is far too amusing and high-spirited to let the play sink into sentimentality.

The questions below will help you to see how Shakespeare produces this blend of comedy and romance that is so enjoyable to watch on the stage.

1 The scene falls into three parts, each with a different comic effect:

190–244
a Rosalind's excitement at learning that Orlando has written the verses.
  i Which speech in particular emphasises her feelings?
  ii What feminine characteristic does Rosalind see herself exhibiting? (Quote the appropriate line if you wish.)

245–284
b The comedy between Orlando and Jaques is based on a witty dialogue in which each character tries to outdo the other in personal insults.
  i Who, in your opinion, wins in this battle of wits?
  ii Quote what you consider to be the best insults.
  iii What is the essential difference between the two characters?

285–407
c This comedy is more truly 'romantic' because it is based on the love between Rosalind and Orlando. Rosalind 'plays the knave' with Orlando and gives free rein to her sense of humour.
  i How does she account for her accent being more polished than that of a shepherd boy?
  ii Can you explain the comic irony of the situation?
  iii How does Rosalind humorously tease Orlando about being in love?

  iv What does she suggest to make sure that she continues to enjoy Orlando's attentions?

2 Using the answers to these questions as your basic material, write a short account of the scene, showing what different types of comedy Shakespeare introduces. Use quotations to illustrate the points you make.

3 The fact that Rosalind retains her sense of humour when she is in love makes her one of the most popular of Shakespeare's heroines. Write a short account of this side of her character as it is depicted in the scene.

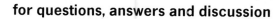

FORUM

for questions, answers and discussion

Is it true that Shakespeare didn't make up his own plots, but took them from other writers? And if it is true, how can he be considered a great original writer if he was using someone else's ideas all the time?

We haven't traced all the sources of the plays, but it's true, Shakespeare didn't invent his own plots. Like most writers of his day, he took them from stories he had read, from history books and even from existing plays. There was an earlier play called 'Hamlet' before Shakespeare's.

But he didn't just copy the stories — he altered them and often wove two or three together to make the plot of his play more intricate and exciting. *A Midsummer Night's Dream* contains three stories cleverly woven together. Then he developed the characters in his own way and gave them depth through his use of language. And he's an *original* writer in the sense that he produced a completely new work of art from the materials he started with. Try reading the poem on which *Romeo and Juliet* is based and then the play itself and you will see what I mean!

● What changes would a writer have to make if he wanted to change a story into a play?

● Which do you think is the most important ingredient of a play — plot, characters or language?

● Does it matter if a plot is 'ridiculous' and you can't believe in it?

Why is Shakespeare considered so 'great' and 'important'? I didn't think much of the television versions of his plays – those I watched, that is. Do you think kids will appreciate him when they have to study a play for an examination – making notes, writing essays, learning quotations!

Not everyone thinks Shakespeare is 'great'. There must be thousands of young people who don't. But he remains popular in the theatre because he produces good dramatic situations, well-drawn characters and fine poetry. He provides juicy parts for actors and actresses and plenty of scope for directors.

You study the plays at school because someone – your teacher or the chief examiner – considers them to be good literature. You may not agree. You may get nothing out of Shakespeare. But you don't know till you've tried, do you? No one will – or should – persuade you that Shakespeare is great; but if you keep reading him and if you can see one or two good performances of his best plays, you might discover it for yourself – who knows?

● Discuss the Shakespeare plays you have seen, on television, in the theatre or cinema. What advantage has one medium over another?
● Are there any advantages in reading a Shakespeare play, as opposed to seeing it performed?
● How would you define a 'great' writer?